Hold Back the Rain

Hold Back the Rain

MICHELLE VIGNAULT

Published by Michelle Vignault Productions, Marietta, GA
www.holdbacktherain.com

Edited and designed by Girl Friday Productions
www.girlfridayproductions.com

Cover design: Emily Weigel
Logo design: Slavko Kahovsky
Project management: Reshma Kooner
Cover photo: Lumiere Tintype Photography

ISBN (paperback): 979-8-218-20427-3
ISBN (ebook): 979-8-218-20598-0

Library of Congress Control Number: 2023909054

For Charlotte and Justine

CONTENTS

Preface 1
Prologue 3

PART ONE: (Reach Up for the) Sunrise 5
PART TWO: My Antarctica 19
PART THREE: What Happens Tomorrow 93
PART FOUR: Do You Realize?? 125
PART FIVE: Save a Prayer 129

Epilogue 139
Acknowledgments 143
About the Author 145

PREFACE

Do you have a friend who understands you completely, someone whom you see day in and day out and who becomes completely integrated into your life before you even realize it? For me, that person is Suzanne. We worked together for over seventeen years at two different jobs. We were there for each other during big life transitions—marriages and divorces, childbirth and birthdays, moving and fender benders, promotions and the loss of those we have loved (including dogs). Heartbreak quickly bonded us, and a lifelong friendship was formed.

My heart has been tested, stomped on, and chewed up. It's been filled with love to the point of overflowing. I've laughed with friends until I couldn't catch my breath; I've cried alone late at night on the kitchen floor, trying to be quiet so as not to wake my girls. I've had the best margaritas on the planet and danced until I dropped. I've cried at funerals and in my car on the way to work. I've cried in hospital rooms, holding my perfect tiny babies as they began their lives, holding the hand of the person I'd promised to love forever as his life ended.

Writing my story has helped me get through what I can only hope will be the hardest years of my life. Many people showed up for me and my family, and to them I will always be grateful. In my very darkest nights, I returned to Suzanne, the best friend a person could have. Through writing letters to her, I found solace.

PROLOGUE

The fluorescent lights buzzed overhead. It could have been anytime, any hospital, anywhere. My footsteps on linoleum, distant beeps of life-sustaining computers, and that ubiquitous buzz were the only sounds. It was almost midnight, Northside Hospital, in Atlanta, Georgia.

Outside, the security lights of the parking lot glowed orange in the cold spring night. Tracy and I had had our first kiss under a security light on our second date, after he'd walked me to my car. It was not all that long ago, and yet it was also a million years ago.

I pulled my cardigan tight around my shoulders, then rooted in my purse for my car keys and the parking pass. My bed was a twenty-minute drive away. If I could just stay awake a little while longer, I could get home, kiss my sleeping daughters good night, and sink down into blessed unconsciousness. I could forget the last two years of a decline I didn't recognize until it was too late, the last fifty days of hurrying and waiting as Tracy lay dying, his liver failing, his body giving out. I could sleep and not dream.

I slid into the driver's seat of our trusty minivan and turned the key in the ignition. How many times had I sat in this very seat, surrounded by crumbs and drained juice boxes and snack wrappers, in traffic or in parking lots, crying and yelling and pounding the steering wheel? Now, there was only silence.

At the empty kiosk, I inserted the parking pass into the

machine and waited for the boom barrier to go up. Nothing. I leaned out the window and pressed the call button.

"Security," said the voice on the other end of the line.

"Hey," I said. "I just put my parking pass in but the arm isn't going up."

A pause. "Yes, it looks like your pass expired at midnight. You owe two dollars."

I looked at the clock on the dash. "It's 12:03," I said.

"Yes. You can repark and go inside to the security desk to pay."

I took a deep breath. "If you don't put this arm up very soon," I said, keeping my tone level, "I will have no problem driving through it."

"Ma'am—"

"MY HUSBAND JUST DIED IN ICU," I screamed. "TRACY FINK. LOOK HIM UP!"

A pause. The boom barrier slowly rose.

Life goes on. I drove home, to my empty bed, my fatherless daughters. Tomorrow was another day.

PART ONE

(REACH UP FOR THE) SUNRISE

Michelle and Tracy get married! June 11, 2011. Photo © Alison Narro

For almost twenty years, I lived in Austin, Texas, a.k.a. Austex—long enough to pass the test given by locals to tell who the "real" Austinites are. "You know Leslie?" a craggy old hippie with a farmer's tan would ask. "Yes" was all I'd have to say to prove my creds. A bearded often-homeless activist who liked wearing tiaras, feather boas, and miniskirts, Leslie was hard to miss. On really hot days, he'd hang around in six-inch heels and a thong. He worked it and he looked good, certainly better than I do in a bikini! He had run for mayor three times on a platform of police accountability and smart residential growth, and he'd become a beloved icon, one of many weird-nesses that kept Austin weird.

Leslie showed up in town a couple of years before I did. I arrived in 1998, straight from Warren Wilson College, in Swannanoa, just outside Asheville, North Carolina. I'd road-tripped through with a college boyfriend and fallen in love with the place and, as my college friends moved far and wide to begin their futures, I chose Austin. My good friend Zeb and her pet tarantula, Sydney, joined me soon thereafter. It was still a somewhat undiscovered town that, like New York City, never sleeps, with some of the best food in the world. It was worth waiting in line for three hours on a Saturday morning to get some of Austin's mouthwatering brisket. I swear, it was so delicious it would bring a tear to my eye.

I lived a few lives in my time there. I was a postcollege

single gal trying to find my place in the world, a marketing and human resources professional, a wife, a divorcée, a parent. The city swaddled me when I needed it and pushed me out of the nest a few times over. A big part of me still feels, will always feel, like an Austinite.

Getting settled into my Texan vibe as a brand-new adult wasn't easy, but my coworker Kathy took me under her wing and out on the town, introducing me to her friends and favorite bars. People there are friendly in that particular central Texas way, and it didn't take too long for me to establish a crew of professional young people looking for a good time. I spent many, many nights dancing to live honky-tonk music and drinking ice-cold Lone Star beer at the Little Longhorn Saloon; on Sundays, we'd play chickenshit bingo, in which owner Ginny would put a large wooden bingo board on one of the pool tables and place a chicken in its center, then secure it with a wire enclosure so it couldn't run off. Wherever the chicken shat was the next letter and number—get five in a row to win! If I was in a festive mood, I'd go to Lala's Little Nugget to celebrate Christmas year-round over garlic knots and paint-peeling-strength rum and Cokes, Bing Crosby crooning "White Christmas" or Eartha Kitt purring "Santa Baby" from the jukebox. Top Notch, a hot-rod hangout straight out of 1971 made even more famous by the cult classic *Dazed and Confused*, was the best spot for ambiance and juicy charcoal-broiled cheeseburgers. In that movie, the bell-bottomed teens hang out at a strip mall with an arcade called the Emporium, which is adjacent to the car shop where Ben Affleck gets his due in the form of a bucket of white paint. I lived behind it on Ruth Avenue.

And then there was Suzanne.

We'd worked together for almost three years at the Eye Clinic of Austin with few exchanges and little conversation between us. She was the LASIK coordinator and surgery assistant, while I was in HR and billing, so we didn't spend much time together, though we saw each other at engagement parties, baby showers, and the monthly bunco games thrown by the other women at the clinic. It wasn't until one fateful day when our paths took a turn to a neighborhood bar called the Boulevard Grill. It was a Thursday afternoon, and we were more than ready for a happy hour. The year was 2001.

We took a seat at a two-top in a darkened corner of the bar, the air conditioner blasting above us, and ordered. Two Lone Stars, please! To hear over the white noise, we had to lean in to talk about her husband, my fiancé, our backgrounds, and general work gossip. Her husband was a comedian who did the kind of drinking that seemed to come with the job. It made sense that she'd be with someone like that, as in an "opposites attract" kind of scenario, given that she seemed to be more on the serious side, at least at first. Over the next few hours, we broke the seal on our friendship and made some big life decisions. No kids for us, no way! Simple times. It was all new and interesting, and before parting ways, we hugged like old friends.

The next day, Suzanne got to work an hour late. She immediately sought me out in the hallway that doubled as a closet, packed with hundreds of files of medical records stacked from floor to ceiling. I stared at her standing in the doorway. While yesterday she'd been animated, flush with discounted beer and good stories, now she was wan, with dark circles under her eyes and not a stitch of makeup. Her fiery red pixie cut, usually pristine, looked frazzled, like she'd tossed and turned in bed all night. I was so surprised that I forgot to use my inside voice or tact. "You look awful," I said. "How much did you drink when you got home?"

"Evidently not enough," Suzanne said. When she had gotten home, she told me, she found her husband waiting for her. "Hi, hon!" she'd said, still happy from our happy hour.

"We need to talk," he said.

"OK . . . ," she said, putting down her purse, those four ominous words ringing in her ears.

He was done with their marriage, he informed her, and wanted to file for a divorce.

Of course, I was sad for Suzanne, but also intrigued. How often do you make a new friend and she comes back the very next day with such life-shattering news? Immediately, I took control. "We'll figure this out," I said, gently steering her toward the back-office door, "but you should definitely not be here. You need to be home so you can cry and hurt and do whatever you need to do. I'll tell the office manager that you had to go home sick."

From then on, I'd check in with her every day at work, asking her how she was holding up as she and her ex split their assets and signed papers. Years passed. Suzanne and her husband officially divorced. I got married. She got a job in the sales team at VisionWeb and brought me in soon thereafter. We turned thirty; I marked the occasion by crying all day until I found out that, no, not everyone had forgotten about my birthday: they'd just been keeping mum until my surprise party. She got remarried and had a baby. I got divorced.

Over the following three years, I realized that it's harder to meet someone you're compatible with after thirty, and simply going out to clubs and bars wasn't going to do the trick. Internet dating was still new and taboo in 2010 but, with some embarrassment, I signed up on OkCupid. That's where I met Tracy Lindell Fink.

I'd just had another sour first and last date when I walked into the Pour House, a hip indoor-outdoor restaurant off Burnet Road. I ordered a beer and carried it outside to look for the tatted strawberry-blond skater boy of the OkCupid profile. I was already flustered by the time I spotted him and made my way over to the table. To my chagrin, he was that perfect combination of sexy and cute, with his trim reddish beard, strong shoulders, and big blue eyes.

Of course, I freaked out. Midway through the first drink, I stood up, mumbled something about needing to let my dogs out, and fled. Later Tracy told me he didn't know what to think of my craziness. But he replied when I texted him that night to apologize, and we decided to go on a date that Wednesday, only three days later. I promised that I would at least finish my drink.

We met at Dart Bowl, a local favorite since 1958, and bowled and laughed for hours. Bowling is such a great way to get to know someone—it's about as casual as can be, you've got a fun, shared activity and plenty of distraction, and you can check out your date while he's taking his turn. After a couple of rounds, he paid the bill and walked me to my car. I had butterflies in my stomach as we left the loud, flashy venue and stepped out into the quiet dusk. In the parking lot, under the one working security light, Tracy kissed me. I was over the moon. After, I watched him cross the street, sure I was going to see him again.

I'm a cautious, organized, tidy person in every avenue of life, except for one: falling in love. Tracy was truly the yang to my yin, a spontaneous thrill-seeker who ran marathons and raced cars, and for him I fell hard. He'd grown up in Kingsville, Texas, a small town built up around the construction of the railroad from Brownsville to St. Louis in the early 1900s. Then came the ranchers and the oil and natural gas industry—today there are still twice as many cattle as people. Tracy's mom was a church secretary; his dad was a laborer. As a scrawny white skater kid with the last name Fink, Tracy had to get tough early on, and the friends he made were for keeps. Back when skateboarding was a true DIY sport, they built a half-pipe in his backyard and practically lived there. I loved that about him, how loyal he was to his hometown friends more than two decades later, and how loyal they were to him.

After one year of dating, we were married, on June 11, 2011. Tracy, like me, had had a starter marriage—his lasted eighteen years—so we planned this casual second wedding using inspiration from Etsy and a brand-new app called Pinterest. He was no more a groomzilla than I was a bridezilla, and I don't recall a single argument. We were also paying for it, so we chose the Mabel Davis Rose Garden at the Zilker Botanical Garden because it cost only $250 to rent the gorgeous oak-shaded space, with a bonus ten chairs thrown into the deal. Part of the bargain was that it was scheduled for three in the afternoon, meaning it would be hellfire hot. That was fine—it's not like we were going to have some long religious ceremony.

Tracy's parents, Tricia and George, and brother, Matthew, made the drive from Bandera, Texas, a two-hour drive from Austin. My brother, Johnny, and his wife, Rowena, flew in from San Francisco. My parents had divorced after forty-six years of marriage, so they took separate flights from Atlanta. My older brother, Mark, traveled with Dad. Suzanne and Shane's kid was our flower child.

I smoothed down my $125 strapless above-the-knee number and double-checked my borrowed diamond necklace, then left the delicious air-conditioning of the main building to step outside into a blast of heat, making my way down the cobblestone steps toward the arch of blush-pink roses. My friend Elizabeth, a seasoned violinist, and her friend Terry played "Only You" by Yazoo as I walked toward Tracy. He stood there smiling, love in his eyes.

Surrounded by forty of our closest friends and family, Reverend Vicki pronounced us husband and wife.

After, we caravanned to Serranos, a Mexican restaurant steps away from the famous Sixth Street strip of clubs, bars, and historic hotels. As predicted, the day had been swelteringly hot, and our guests enjoyed cold water, colder margaritas, and the buffet of sizzling fajitas and enchiladas in our reserved room in the back. Everyone cheered and waved as we got into the pedicab that was waiting for us at the end of the party and set off on the three-mile ride to our hotel. Tracy and I held hands and giggled about nothing as we headed northwest on Sixth Street, passing the state capitol to the right, and turned left onto Congress Avenue. At the Congress Avenue Bridge over Lady Bird Lake, locals and tourists were lined up to watch the bats fly out from under the bridge and over the tree line in search of their insect dinner. This was something I had experienced countless times over with visiting friends or alone on walks to take in the shimmering downtown view.

The last mile was pretty much straight uphill, and we offered to hop off to give the rickshaw guy a break, but he wasn't having it. He was dripping sweat by the time we pulled into the driveway of the Hotel San José. Our weeklong honeymoon to Isla Mujeres, Mexico, awaited us the next day.

***

Between June 2011 and the summer of 2014, a lot happened to us as a couple. For two people who hadn't wanted kids, we sure did get busy. I was nearing forty, and Tracy had just passed that milestone. For our first child, I set up a home bathroom spa experience with candles and calming music as my contractions began, until my water broke and we left for the hospital. Our birthing instructor recommended bringing a photo to focus on during labor, and I stared at the painting of the cutest little dog named Frieda I'd found at a thrift store as I huffed and puffed. Charlotte arrived in November of 2012—that painting of Frieda now lives in her bedroom. Twenty months later, in July of 2014, we celebrated the birth of our second daughter,

Justine. She popped out with a Joan Jett–punk head of black hair. She was unique from day one and has made me laugh every day since.

As summer turned to fall, we made a big decision. Austin had stopped feeling like our little secret, a small town with the best of a big city. For one, our car was stolen out of our driveway during a night in October. There's no confusion like the kind of confusion you have when you go outside to make your commute and the car you left there the previous evening is just . . . gone. Even though what had happened was obvious, it took us a little while to figure it out. (The police found our Jeep about three weeks later, parked between two houses as the thief burgled one of them. The good news? The insurance company had already cut a check, and we got to keep the money, hunny! Got ourselves a new ride.)

Tracy's best guy friends had already begun the exodus out of Austin and, with the increasing cost of living and crazy traffic, we'd decided it was time for us to leave, too. His job as a global financial analyst had been stable, but the boss whom he'd followed to General Electric had just left the company, and now Tracy wasn't sure what might happen. I came up with a list of reasons to go to Georgia: My parents had reached their eighties and though my brother Mark lived near them, he'd long had his own struggles with mental illness and couldn't be relied on should they need help. The school system was a better match for our family. Also, I missed seasons.

Destination: Atlanta.

And so Tracy quit his job and we put our house on the market. The CFO of my company, sensing change in the air, asked if I'd consider working remote. Over eleven years, Suzanne and I had created a dedicated sales and support team that we cared a great deal about, and we enjoyed a fantastic amount of flexibility, with free rein and no one breathing down our necks. But as it does when companies grow, the culture was shifting, and many of us old-timers were beginning to look for greener pastures. "No, thank you," I said. "We have a plan for once we get to Georgia."

***

I met up with Suzanne at the Workhorse, a true Texan bar on North Loop, across the street from Room Service Vintage, to give her the news. We got some beers—I ordered an Austin Amber, already nostalgic for local beer—and eyed the menu. The white wings, chicken wings wrapped in bacon and stuffed with jalapeños, with both wing sauce and ranch dipping sauce, looked good. But no, I wasn't hungry, not really. We sat inside at one of the rudimentary wooden tables and looked at each other.

"I have something to tell you," Suzanne said, just as I said, "I have something to tell you." We laughed.

"You go first," I said.

She smiled and took a gulp of beer. "I got my real estate license."

I raised my glass and she clinked hers against it. "Cheers to you!"

"Thank you. Shane and I have been talking about it, and we've decided that I can't really work full-time at VisionWeb if I want to get my real estate business going. So I'm giving notice."

"I'm so happy for you. You're going to kill it as a real estate agent."

"That's the plan. OK, now you go."

"Well, funny you should mention giving notice. Because I'm also giving my notice."

"Did you get a new job?"

"No . . . we're moving to Atlanta!"

Suzanne's face fell for just a second. "You're moving?"

"Our mortgage is going up, and cost of living is just getting too crazy here. Plus, I want to be closer to my parents."

"Even Walter?"

Suzanne was not the biggest fan of my dad. "Well, you know," I said. "My folks are divorced now, and I'd really like my kids to get to spend more time with their grandparents."

Suzanne nodded. Her mom's health was deteriorating, and she knew firsthand how hard it was to take care of an ailing parent and a child at the same time. "What do you have lined up for work?"

Now I took a gulp of my beer. Suzanne was one of those true-blue friends whom you could count on to tell it like it is, a habit I loved her for and that, at the same time, occasionally made me think twice before dishing. Not that I'm a big blabber anyway. But I knew that this news would probably throw her off. For our entire friendship, for the going on fifteen years we'd worked together, she'd known me as reliable and organized, someone who pretty much always has her ducks in a row. Fastidious even. I was not someone who jumped off cliffs. "We don't have work lined up yet," I told her. "We're going to stay at my mom's for a few months while she's traveling. That'll give us time for Tracy to find something. I've always wanted to stay at home with the girls, and this'll be my chance."

Suzanne blinked. I braced myself. I could recognize that this was a little out of character for me, but Tracy and I had made the decision, and the momentum of that was already carrying us forward. For once in my life, I didn't want to hear it, didn't want my brash decision to be questioned, even in the most loving way. I could see the wheels turning in her head, but after a pause, she said, "Wow, that's crazy! I'm . . . I'm surprised you're going to move without a job!" And that was it.

***

We spent the last few weeks of 2014 packing and prepping our house to sell. Suzanne and her husband kindly let us stay at their place with their dog, Loretta, while they were in Cozumel for Christmas break. Austin had long been a seller's market, even when the housing bubble popped in 2008 and the rest of the country's real estate sunk underwater. We put our house on the market assuming it'd be snapped up in a flash but, as day four came and went, we were seriously stressing out. We needed that money. It finally sold and, with a sigh of relief, we started saying our goodbyes and eating at as many of our favorite restaurants as possible. We got the breakfast tacos and migas plate at Habanero's, Rosie's famous tamales and the chicken enchiladas with Spanish sauce at Rosie's Tamales House, and a couple of baskets of fried chicken with a side of West Texas red chili at Lucy's. I held back tears unrelated to the spiciness at Habanero's on South First and Oltorf (I can still taste their migas plate with a fizzy Coca-Cola on the side). Though Tracy was excited, it was hard for him, too—he'd only ever lived in Texas. I'd spent twenty years in the Lone Star State (with a slight detour to Brooklyn, New York, for two years) and loved it for most of that time, but I was ready to go home.

As the year came to a close, we loaded up our van with two dogs, two toddlers, and two semiadults.

Our plan? To figure it out when we got there.

PART TWO

MY ANTARCTICA

Atlanta, here we come! January 2, 2015. Photo © Michelle Vignault

January 1, 2015
Happy New Year, Suzanne. I hope yours is off to a better start than mine.

We've made it to our first stop, in New Orleans. I miss you already, and so I'm going to write you letters and pretend like we're drinking beer and chatting and nibbling on brisket, like we used to do before life got so complicated.

It feels like things have already changed since we left Austin, and not in a good way. We spent our first day walking around the city, eating beignets and drinking coffee as the girls took in all the sights and sounds. Well, I drank coffee; Tracy drank vodka and Gatorade over ice in a supersize gas station cup. "We're on vacation!" he said. You know me—I'm not so good at vacation. For all my bravado with our former boss, I was already worrying about where we were going to live and how Tracy was going to find a job in Atlanta. Maybe our "plan" wasn't so great after all. But Tracy was right. The whole point was that we would be OK as long as we were together, and the pieces would fall into place if we (I) could relax and just let them.

After a long day, we went up to our fancy, pet-friendly king suite and tucked the girls in. They fell asleep right away, and thank goodness they did, because Tracy was in a mood. It's kind of hard to describe. He was just . . . unreasonable. Irritated and pushy, but without any specific issue to address. Almost like when a little kid gets overtired, and there's nothing you can do but go along with it until they fully tucker themselves out. Honestly, I've never seen him that way before. My tactic of nonengagement didn't work, and it quickly escalated to a stupid fight over pretty much nothing. Something about when we'd leave NOLA for the next part of the drive. Not a big deal, right? But he couldn't let it go. I was lying in bed, trying to signal that the fight was over, we should just call it a day and go to sleep, and we'd figure it out in the morning. He was standing beside the bed, hovering over me, getting way too close, all up in my face. I was panicking. I'd never felt physically threatened before by him, but in that moment, I was afraid to move, that I'd do something wrong and he'd lash out. It reminded me of my dad back in the day, when he'd get in a tizzy and start yelling at my mom, and I'd slink off or get as small and quiet as possible, hoping it'd pass. Now I couldn't slink off, obviously, and I had the girls to think about. Tracy was yelling and waving his finger in my face, and I was trying to shush him. Last thing we needed was to wake up Charlotte and Justine or to have someone complain to the hotel about the noise.

He was just . . . mean. Angry and mean. Eventually I realized that my lying there wasn't calming him, so I sat up and tried to push him away. He stepped back and I fell out of bed and onto the floor, landing on my hip. That startled him. "We're done," I shout-whispered, nearly crying. He didn't say anything, but that put an end to our fight.

The next day, I was an exhausted mess with my head in a fog, and Tracy was hungover. I'm not sure if he even remembered what had happened. We didn't talk about it. Two dogs and two kids needed our attention, and so we just focused on them. Not the best way to begin our new life, but I'm glad it's over, and I hope we can forget it and move on.

Sigh,

Michelle

January 4, 2015

Pooky,

We made it to Atlanta, timing it so that we got to Mom's house in the burbs right before she goes on her big three-month cruise to East Asia, including Singapore and India. Can you imagine traveling for that long? How awesome. I don't blame her for not wanting to deal with the six of us, and she's earned it, what with raising me and my brothers and dealing with my dad for all those years, only to get divorced forty-six years in. Forty-six years! I can't imagine how they put up with each other for so long.

This setup is great as it'll give us a rent-free place to stay while we find a house and Tracy gets a job. I'm excited to be a stay-at-home mom for a little while, to do all those things I was too busy to do in Austin. Make sandwiches and go on picnics at Morgan Falls Park, spend rainy afternoons at the library, have dance parties and then quiet time while the girls go down for long afternoon naps. I admit some of my fantasies are kind of *Leave It to Beaver*: Tracy getting home from work, loosening his tie, and coming into the kitchen to give me a kiss on the cheek as I prep some gourmet something or other for dinner. (Ha! As if.) Who knew I had a 1950s housewife inside me all this time, just waiting to get out?

We figure that between now and the time the girls start kindergarten, my staying home will balance out the cost of day care. I can always pick my career back up where I left off. Anyway, you did it with your kid and that seemed to work well for your family. I learn from the best!

Love you,

Michelle

February 2, 2015

Suzanne,

I miss you so much! Life has been crazy, but it's nice to be back in Atlanta. With my mom away on her grand tour, seeing my dad and his girlfriend, Sandy, is a little bit easier. My parents live only about ten minutes apart, but they are definitely not on amicable terms. I've been visiting with my brother Mark, too, seeing him more than I have since he went off to college when I was ten or so. Well, minus the year he spent with us when we lived in France. Anyway, they are so happy to have Charlotte and Justine nearby, being the doting grandpa and uncle that they've been able to be for only a week or two at a time these last few years. Mark, especially, is all hugs and kisses. He's in one of his quiet states, neither on a manic high or a depressive low. More like a wintertime hibernation, which is actually very peaceful to be around. He'll be like, "Give me that child!" and then hold the girls for as long as they'll let him. It's really very sweet.

Keep Austin weird in my absence,

M

June 13, 2015

Suzanne,

Can you believe I haven't written in *so* long? We've spent the last six months living off the insurance money for our stolen car and the sale of our house and attempting to get settled and start the next phase of the Fink/Vignault family. I've been showing Tracy and the girls around the city, which is practically new to me since it's been so long since I lived here. As hoped, we've taken the girls to the park, the library, all that nice, fun kid stuff. Of course, we have to do the more stressful grown-up stuff, too. It took us the full three months that my mom was gone for us to find a rental—apparently two people with no jobs, no credit history in the state of Georgia, two kids, and two dogs are no one's idea of good rental candidates. We finally found something, though the location isn't ideal.

Where our street, Brantley Road, meets an arterial called Roswell Road is the Sandy Springs Gun Range, which just so happens to be the place where my brother Mark buys his guns. The house itself is a little strange, sprinkled with random design choices that were clearly made based on price point, with a main space like an alleyway going from the kitchen to the dining room to the living room to a sunroom with floor-to-ceiling windows. The basement is down these rickety old steps, with a little dungeon of a bedroom and a bathroom that was clearly thrown together with no plan and using the cheapest materials available. No one likes to go down there except Luci and Mackey, who use it as a thoroughfare to get to the backyard. There's a random red wall in the dining room, and the entire upstairs is carpeted in the brightest green I've ever seen. Like golf course green. Who in their right mind would choose a Kelly-green carpet for the upstairs bedrooms? Tiger Woods? The place's saving grace is the amount of space and light, which feels especially nice after cramping my mom's style for the last few months. We had to pay for six months up front, plus the application fee and the extra pet fees. There went a big chunk of our savings, but at least that's one less thing to worry about for a little while.

We've also had to face the fact that, yes, I'm bossy. It's not easy for me to sit back and let Tracy do the job hunt his way. If it were me, I would have been ready to get out there from the get-go. He took his sweet time. I think maybe he got too comfortable in vacation mode, while I'm biting my nails as our bank account dwindles. Finally, I sat down with him to work on his LinkedIn profile and his résumé and to help him with online job postings. It was like pulling teeth—the man just doesn't like tech. Well, too bad, that's the world we live in. Things were tense for a while, but Tracy found a job! It's in finance, for a large corporation, as he's used to, and the location is great, only fifteen minutes away from our rental and essentially off the main road where we live. We're incredibly excited to be over this hurdle.

I miss you. When do you think you can come visit? Soon, you think?

Hugs to the three of you,
Michelle

June 27, 2015

Pooky,

Well, son of a bitch. Knowing that a paycheck was in our near future lifted some of the pressure off us, but after a week, I could tell something was not right with Tracy. A wife knows.

I waited until the following week to ask him about it. He was sitting on the couch, suit jacket thrown over the armrest, shoes kicked off and feet up on the coffee table, fresh drink in hand. The Fink Family Special: ice, Gatorade, vodka.

"You don't seem all that happy with your new job," I said, trying to keep things light and to let him know that I'm on his side. Yes, I want him to work. Scratch that—*we need* him to work. But lately it's felt like we're adversaries, not partners. Oddly, I am getting pushback about helping him find a different job. I know we have different goals, though of course we both want what's best for the family. Maybe it's just that we have different styles for making things happen.

"I don't understand why they hired me," he said. Then he took a big gulp from his Big Gulp cup, ice knocking against the plastic. "I think it was to fulfill some requirement or something."

"What gives you that idea?"

He rolled his eyes. "They've parked me in a hallway, with people walking back and forth by my desk all day long. How am I supposed to get anything done?" Another big gulp, more shaking ice. "And my boss doesn't seem to know what my actual role is."

"That sounds really hard," said Mrs. Understanding Wife. "Maybe they just need some time to figure out your role and where to put you?"

He shrugged. My chest got really tight. I knew he wasn't going to be patient, and I can't comprehend why. It's like he's not taking our financial situation seriously, or he doesn't care. Our money is running out. We need this job. We need this job. We need this job. My stress level is off the charts, girl.

Sigh,

Michelle

July 15, 2015

Pooky,

I cannot believe my baby girl is one year old! What a first year Justine has had. We took her in for her one-year checkup, even though we don't have insurance. But you know as much as anyone that, when you have kids, you'll do just about anything to make sure they're healthy and happy. If something seems off then you address it, you do your best to fix whatever needs fixing. All that to say that something is going on with Justine, and I'm pretty sure a Band-Aid or a kiss on the head is not going to cut it.

There are a few things that, if they were happening alone, wouldn't be a big deal. But in combination, it could add up to something that we need to take care of now, sooner rather than later, health insurance or no health insurance. For one, Justine's a head banger. I've read online that this is pretty common, but she bangs her head a lot or, at least, more than we like. On top of that, she's not standing or walking. Maybe we're getting ahead of ourselves worrying about walking, but she doesn't seem to have an interest in standing up. She doesn't pull herself up by holding on to the edge of the couch or on to my leg, even with coaxing. To get around, she'll do the monkey scoot, sort of on one knee and dragging one of her legs behind her. OK, so fine, not the end of the world. Except she hasn't attempted any sort of verbalization either. No "mama" or "dada" or "baba." Again, not the end of the world on its own. And as much as we don't want to be the type of parents who let developmental milestones rule our lives—or, heaven forbid, the type of parents who brag about their kids' mastery of the ABCs or their early potty training or whatever at the playground—we also want to be sure Justine is making progress. If she needs help, then we'll get her help.

Tracy and I are able to come together and have a real conversation, without anger or bitterness, on this one crucial thing. Why is our baby not trying? Why can't she stand or walk?

We were sad to leave our favorite pediatrician in Austin, and we were NOT happy with the local one here in chichi East Cobb, no matter the number of recommendations we got. The doctor we saw basically diagnosed at first sight. Autism. It's not that we hadn't thought of that possibility, or that we're in some kind of denial. If that's what we're dealing with, then that's what we'll deal with. It's that he walked into the exam room, we listed the things we were worried about, and he proclaimed his edict from on high without even examining the patient or asking follow-up questions.

What the fuck? This is modern medicine at its finest? My heart and gut are telling me that that is not it, but no one is listening to me. Apparently, the doctor was not used to mothers debating his diagnoses, and I started to get worked up. Then the nurse asked me to calm down—No, ma'am!—and suggested I get a second opinion if I didn't like theirs. Which is exactly what we did.

Then, after spending a million hours getting on Medicaid, we were able to visit another pediatrician who DID THE SAME THING! Walked in, asked about symptoms, and diagnosed, all within ten minutes. Totally disengaged. When we pressed again, the explanations were vague. Justine is not a case study or a cardboard cutout of a kid, I wanted to remind them; she's a living, breathing little lovebug who deserves real attention. Whatever is going on with her, we simply want her diagnosed accurately. And we are not ready to chart her as autistic yet. Maybe someday, after someone who cares takes a good long look at her. But not yet. Very simple.

So we kept looking. Side note: Medicaid has some of the best benefits we've ever had. Under typical insurance, Tracy's blood pressure medicine was thirty dollars per month. On Medicaid it's fifty cents per month. For the same medication? Geesh.

Finally, we found Babies Can't Wait, a statewide early intervention program that serves babies and toddlers with developmental delays and disabilities. They sent a caseworker to the house to meet us and do a real evaluation as part of the program intake. She spent an hour and a half with Justine, just playing with her and observing and taking notes. Unlike the doctors, she did not seem to be bored or in a rush, and she made no indication of a diagnosis before she was good and ready, instead focusing not on a label but what we could actually *do*. Together we decided that twice weekly physical therapy, occupational therapy, and/or speech therapy appointments would be the best route to helping our girl with hand movements, grip, walking and motor skills, muscle memory, and verbal skills.

A miracle, a light at the end of the tunnel. A real plan, focused on helping this unique person with her unique challenges. To say we've cried some is an understatement. But, today at least, instead of tears of confusion or frustration, Tracy and I cried with relief. Our baby is going to get the help she needs. Some good karma has arrived for our family of four. Alright, alright, alright, we make six with the dogs.

Love you,
Michelle

October 8, 2015

Pooky,

Justine has started her program, and Tracy has surprised me by leading the charge. Sometimes the four of us go to her appointments but often Charlotte and I will stay home or go to the park or grocery store while he takes Justine. They bring back homework, little tasks or activities to keep up the work between sessions. We're helping her with her habits and posture, encouraging her to stand upright at every opportunity. We'll turn on cartoons and plunk her down so she's standing, leaning against the couch, which she seems to enjoy, and we bring her little pushcart with us to the park so that she can stand and walk with assistance. Charlotte has been great, taking it upon her three-year-old self to help her little sissy. She's nurturing like that and doesn't seem to mind the extra attention Justine's been getting lately. It's so sweet.

Love,

M

October 11, 2015

Dear Pooky,

More good news. I was accepted into the docent program at the High Museum of Art or, as locals call it, the High. I don't know if I ever told you, but I had dreams of being a museum curator back when I was in college, and I interned at the High over one summer break. Obviously, my path took another turn, but since I'm not working, I'm going to volunteer as a docent. So far, the class is great. It's on Wednesdays from 10:00 a.m. to 2:00 p.m., and there are about thirty other people who are equally nerdy about art and the High. You have to be able to commit to an unpaid gig in the middle of the workday, so most of the other aspiring docents are retired folks, but there is a guy named Matt, who looks to be about our age. We hit it off right away while waiting in the lobby before the first day of class. Besides our shared youth (youth being relative here) and passion for art, we both wore Doc Martens. That's enough to spark a conversation, and we ended up sitting together in class. Turns out we both take the MARTA into the city, so we plan on meeting at the train stop next week.

October 29, 2015
Pooky,

It's so nice being able to get away and make a friend with whom I can have adult conversations. Fun conversations that have nothing to do with unemployment or who's going to take out the trash. Matt and I have started a tradition of getting off the train on Wednesday mornings and taking a short walk to a nearby Starbucks, where we pick up coffee we've ordered off the app. This is a rare treat for me, given how Tracy and I are counting our pennies, but soooo worth it. We show up on time like the good students we are, coffee piping hot and pencils sharp. And check it out! The museum gave us employee badges. I'm so official!

I love learning about the art exhibits—their creators, their histories, their influences, their cultural significance. There's this one piece I'm kind of obsessed with. It's this big mirrored bowl by Anish Kapoor, like a large disco ball cut in half. When you stand in front of it, your reflection is pixelated and bounced back and forth in this trippy way. I could stand there forever.

On the train ride home the other day, I learned that Matt has two sons and he's a widower. In the late aughts, his wife moved away to tackle her own mental illness but ended up taking her life. The boys were young, just starting out in elementary school at the time.

So sad. Not that you'd know Matt's had this tragic past by looking at him—he's one of those chatty, happy-go-lucky guys. We could talk all day about art, music, food, relationships, sex. This man is not shy. The docent crew already thinks we're an item, but don't worry. Hello, I'm married with two kids at home, and he's got a sometimes girlfriend. So no monkey business, just fun weekly conversation and some hot coffee.

M

January 2, 2016

Dear Suzanne,

I'm so relieved that 2015 is over. Last year was challenging, to say the least. We knew moving to Atlanta would be tough but not this tough. I shouldn't be surprised that it's been hard to make friends, given that we're not involved in the things that come with built-in community, like church or day care. People are friendly and all, but it takes a while to get past talking weather at the playground. Fortunately, we've found a family of four with kids the same ages as the girls.

This past fall, we signed up Charlotte for soccer on Saturday mornings. Tracy and I would sit in the stands with Justine while this gaggle of three-year-olds chased after a ball. Charlotte loved it, and it was beyond cute, all those kids falling over and getting distracted by birds and mud and who knows what else and just doing their funny kid antics.

On the very last Saturday, we were walking to our car when this couple runs over and introduces themselves. Tanairis and Tim. I'd noticed their son, Thomas, and Charlotte playing together out on the field, and the parents taking turns keeping their younger child occupied. Tanairis was like, "Hey, I think our kids get along. Do you want to be friends?"

Who knew, after all those lonely months, it could be that easy? We've had some playdates at the playground and gone to dinner at this little pizzeria near the soccer field and gotten to know them better since then. Justine and Savannah hit it off immediately, and we joke about how Charlotte and Thomas are going to get married someday. It's been wonderful having some real-live grown-ups to talk to, and it feels like at least one tiny piece of our lives is getting a little bit settled.

Still, there's the work issue. It's been nuts here, and I have yet to tell you that Tracy quit his job. Outside of a two-week stint, we've been without income for an entire year. A year! Just writing that makes my heart rate spike. At first, I was helping Tracy get his online presence in order, but at a certain point I decided that it would just be easier if I did it for him. Perhaps I let my Virgo self run a little wild. But of course, my process is better! You know exactly what I'm talking about. Don't you and I always have the best ideas? So, OK, I went over his head and reached out to his contacts for job leads. I even found an organization that will help with résumés and photos for your online profile, all for free, but he couldn't be bothered to go to their event. And yes, I filled out job-search site applications on his behalf. I mean, he has this killer résumé. All I'm doing is putting it out there. Senior financial analyst for GE and for Rockwell Software, which had an annual revenue of $5 billion to $7 billion while he was there. Billion, with a B! Evergreen skills like accounting and payroll and billing. He even won an award for outstanding achievement in 2000, in his first job at Trilogy. Why, you may be wondering, am I telling you all this? Because I need to remind myself what he's capable of. Not that I was necessarily looking for a "good earner," but when we first met, he was doing really well. He worked hard, he played hard, just like me. That's why this inertia is so baffling. It's like he's forgotten who he used to be, or he no longer cares. Or he's OK with me taking on everything.

I know, I know, my manhandling is not great. But there are a million freaking jobs out there for him, and he's just not motivated to go and get one.

At least we've managed to stick to a tight budget all year. Not that big of a deal. Our one splurge is a monthly or bi-monthly visit to Chuy's for Tex-Mex happy hour, to give the girls a taste of central Texas and, I hope, to make Tracy feel at home (and to shake him out of the funk he's in). It was even founded in Austin in the early eighties, and it's got a cool vibe, with framed photos of dogs everywhere—bring a pic of your pup and you get a free dessert. We get a couple of margaritas made with fresh-squeezed limes and then take the girls to the open salsa bar, where you can get unlimited chips and the best creamy jalapeño dipping sauce in the world. They order the kids' menu burritos or quesadillas and are in seventh heaven. As we crunch our chips and drink our drinks, all the pressures and conflicts recede for an hour or two. Tracy is in his happy place and we can ignore everything else and have fun, real fun, minimal faking involved. It costs a chunk of change for us even at happy hour prices, but the break from life is so worth it. Those dinners are some of my best memories from this very tense year.

Now that the holidays are over, I can tell you that this has been one of the saddest seasons of my life. I hung up Christmas decorations from years past, and I made a garland with the many greeting cards that arrived in the mail, including the one you sent us. We unboxed the gifts from friends and from Granny and Papa in Texas and wrapped them up for Santa to leave under our small fake tabletop Christmas tree. The girls were thrilled Christmas morning—they didn't know that none of the presents came from Mommy and Daddy. Meanwhile, Tracy and I could barely look at each other. We had no money for gifts for each other, nothing to open, no gestures of love to exchange.

Thank goodness for Charlotte and Justine. They were practically bouncing off the walls with happiness. Granny sent a little pink kitchen, and the girls have spent the last week playing with it. Justine likes to hold the spatula and lean on her sister, while Charlotte stands at the little stove proudly whipping up an imaginary dinner. It's a joy to watch them in action.

I'll try to remember that as part of my New Year's resolution, to find the silver lining, no matter how dark it gets. This year can only get easier, right?

I love you lots,

M

February 6, 2016

Suzanne,

I haven't written in a while because I wanted to give you some space. OK, that's a lie. I'm afraid you're going to say, "I told you so." Not that you would do that, but still. Finding those silver linings this past month has been nearly impossible. The one thing I take pride in is that we still haven't asked our families for money. I'm too embarrassed. My parents have been so great, helping out with the kids and in so many other ways. My mom is her usual dependable self, showing up for us when we need her, changing diapers and going on adventures to the park. I've told her a little bit about what's going on with Tracy, and she doesn't judge, just lets me cry on her shoulder. My mom is amazing.

I don't talk to my dad much about what's happening. Part of it is that I don't think he can sympathize or relate. That's just not in his emotional tool belt, so what's the point? Part of it is that I'm stubborn, and I hate to disappoint. I've kept my beeswax to myself for so long, and I like it that way. I was the good girl, the one kid who held her shit together most of the time, especially when Mark was having his troubles or Johnny was being cranky. To be a disappointment to my dad would be crushing.

Anyway, at the end of the day, we don't really need to have a heart-to-heart, because things are working between us. I'm actually a little confused by how great my dad is being. When I was growing up, he was the classic disciplinarian dad, loud and temperamental and scary. He said jump and we'd jump. But now he's this calm, patient grandpa who sits on the floor with Justine or takes the girls to McDonald's. (Johnny was so jealous when he heard about that. "Dad never sat on the floor and played with us!" he said.) If they want chocolate milk, then, by George, he's going to get them chocolate milk. As far as I can remember, he never took us to the pool, but he takes the girls there all the time. Maybe it's just easier being a grandparent, when you don't have to worry about all the minutia and the responsibility of raising kids. You can be loving and silly and then hand them back to the parents when a diaper is dirty or a tantrum is coming on. Maybe my dad has just gotten a little more jovial with age. Maybe a part of him knows he wasn't the best hands-on father in the world and, instead of admitting outright to any kind of failing or mistake, he's getting a redo, making up for lost time. Whatever the reason, I'll take it.

As for Tracy's family . . . they don't have much extra to give but, more than that, his mom is still mad that we moved. She threw a huge fit when we told them, saying that we were taking her grandkids away, how could we hurt her this way, that kind of thing. Very dramatic. She vowed to never come visit us in Georgia, and so far, she's stuck to her word.

Financially speaking, we've made our bed and now we're lying in it. Valentine's Day isn't looking too promising, especially now that I've made the decision to let go of my stay-at-home-mom dreams and find work. Someone's got to pay the bills, and if Tracy's not going to do it, I will. When I told him that I planned to get a job within a month, he literally laughed in my face.

Challenge accepted, MF. Let the games begin.

M

March 10, 2016
Suzanne,

Since I last wrote to you, every waking moment that I have

not been with the girls, I have been tweaking my résumé, applying for jobs, networking, calling former bosses to ask about leads in Atlanta. I applied for jobs I was way overqualified for and jobs I was completely underqualified for. The last time I job searched was over sixteen years ago! A lot has changed, and now we're in a different city. Honestly, I have been begging. It's not a good look, but I really don't care—I'm covering all my bases.

The other day I got a return call from a small tech support company. For the first time ever, I was asked to do the pen sell in my phone interview. Have you heard of this? I had to look up what the hell human resources was even talking about. There's that famous scene in *The Wolf of Wall Street*, where the sleazy stockbroker goes around to people in the audience and says, "Sell me this pen." The point is that it's not about how great the pen is, it's about finding out what the potential buyer is looking for in a pen and establishing rapport. The idea being that, if you have rapport, you can sell anything. Ugh. It was painful, but apparently, I must not have sucked too bad because they hired me! It's only a part-time job, but still! Only took me six weeks to get it. Boom, MF!

OMG—good news!

Michelle

March 30, 2016

Pooky,

To say I've been in a better mood lately is putting it mildly. I have never been so excited to get up early in the morning and go to work. I miss the girls, of course, but I'm so glad to get out of the house and, if I'm being honest, away from Tracy. You know what the first thing he said to me was when I told him the good news about the job? "Why bother?" That's it. So, fine, it's a part-time job with no benefits, but it's better than nothing, which is all he's got to offer these days. I can understand why he's frustrated, but at the same time I could use a little support, even encouragement. Instead, my working is just another reason for him to be resentful. I'm really, really tired of him taking his frustration out on me.

The company hired me for an entry-level sales job despite their own reservations about me. Mostly they were afraid that I'd jump ship as soon as I found a better opportunity. "I'm not interested in a full-time job," I told them, straight-up lying through my teeth. "I'm simply looking to learn from you and make a little money." Every minute I wasn't working, however, I was in fact looking for a full-time job with benefits. Sorry, small software company, but mama bear has mouths to feed. In the end, they were right. I quit after three weeks when I received a life-changing phone call. I don't want to jinx it by talking about it too soon, so I'll just say this: fingers crossed!

Wish me luck,

Michelle

April 15, 2016

Suzanne,

A few days ago, after fifteen years with her, I had to put Luci down. My little pound puppy, who pushed ahead of the other puppies in the crate to get to the front. It was love at first sight. Christian and I had just gotten married, and we took her home and pretty quickly landed on a name: Lucifer J. She did not listen, did not obey, barked at everyone no matter how many times they'd come to the door. She was the cutest little demon dog and the world's best snuggler, there for me through the divorce, during my toughest times. But, as you know, she's been slowing down, and it became clear when she lost her appetite and her desire to go for walks that the end was near.

My heart is breaking. The drive home from the vet's was quiet; for once Tracy and I weren't fighting. We both just cried. I've been crying nonstop ever since. I've been crying for

Mackey, who just lost his best friend. Luci was not the best-behaved dog, but she was who she was. I hope she knew how much we loved her.

Michelle

April 30, 2016
Suzanne,

I am ready to share with you my good news about this new job. My new boss, Rick, and an amazing woman named Karen called me at a time when I was desperate, and even though I am not familiar with the utility tech industry, they decided to take a chance on me. I am so incredibly grateful to them, and I'm determined to learn everything I can and make sure they don't regret hiring me for this sales role.

My interview was almost three hours long. We even went to lunch midway through, and at the very end, as I was walking out of the office, Karen and I lingered to chat. It was like we were old friends. She was so warm. We laughed and laughed and finally, when it was really time to go, one of us said, "Should we hug?" Then we laughed some more. You don't do that at a job interview, right? I passed all their tests, calls, and questions and began working full-time soon after. Did I mention that we'll be getting HEALTH INSURANCE?!?!

The Clearion office is quickly becoming my sanctuary. The kids are still in bed and Tracy is still snoring on the couch when I leave in the morning. I kiss the girls goodbye and sneak out, afraid that I'll wake up Tracy, whose resentment and jealousy has only gotten worse with this fantastic, lifesaving development. Isn't that strange? My success is the family's success, or at least that's how I see it. I guess he sees it differently. It seems to make him more insecure, like my employment is a statement on his level of competence rather than a true godsend for all of us. He's turning inward, turning into this silent, brooding person that is so far removed from the Austin version of Tracy that I can hardly recognize him. Do you remember when he took me and Charlotte on that trip to Chicago, when I was six months pregnant with Justine? Justin Timberlake was performing at the United Center, and Tracy got us a hotel room, then spent two hours running around downtown searching for the best deep-dish pizza Chicago had to offer. I went off with my big belly to the concert while he tucked in Charlotte, and the next day we visited the Bean and the Art Institute of Chicago. That was such a fun trip, with Tracy in full loving-papa mode.

Where'd that guy go? I think maybe he's ashamed. I get that he feels "stuck" at home, even though, in my opinion, that was his choice. (He's not the first person to feel a little stifled by the homemaker role. I want to say to him, "Ever heard of Betty Friedan? *The Feminine Mystique*? Bored housewives popping pills and downing martinis and dreaming about running off with the door-to-door vacuum salesman? Um, second-wave feminism, hello?") Tracy has yet to congratulate me on landing this full-time job with benefits that our family so needs, and he hasn't asked me anything about it. He doesn't ask me about my new responsibilities or my training. He doesn't ask about my new coworkers, lovely people who've gone out of their way to welcome me and show me around. Nothing.

As I drive down the highway in the mornings, I scream in the car. I must look like a madwoman, but I have to vent my frustration somehow. Then I sit in the parking lot for a few minutes to check my mascara and smooth out my hair and collect myself before going inside. I feel like I'm an actress on the red carpet by the time I get to my desk—my job is the award I've won, and I'm smiling big. I am truly beyond excited, but I have to compartmentalize, setting aside my personal life so I can get to work. After this past year and a half of sweating over every penny, I feel like a million bucks just grabbing lunch with my team. The office is just off Buford Highway and in an area known for its eclectic cuisine. We often walk to a local Cuban restaurant called Havana Sandwich Shop. I have become a huge fan of their flaky Cuban sandwich, and Karen and I usually share an order of chicken-and-cheese empanadas. Delish. And don't get me started on the Malaysian curry laksa chicken noodle soup at the Food Terminal a bit farther down the road. Can I have menu item NS08, please?

I am happy to work my tail off, more than happy to call home to tell Tracy that I "have to" work late. Even though things are so bad between us, I know that Charlotte and Justine are in good hands. He reserves his fun and spontaneous side for them, while I get only anger. Every time I walk in the door, I wonder what I'll be stepping into and hope that we can at least pretend to be civil in front of the girls. Sad to say, but the less I'm home, the happier the home is for them.

Remember after our wedding reception at the Mexican restaurant, when Tracy and I were sitting in the pedicab, waving as we left for our hotel? The sound of Lone Star beer cans tied to the back rattling on the street. I remember sitting snuggled close, feeling so filled with love, so over the moon to be with this man. I miss those feelings.

Looks like I've caught the nostalgia bug tonight. At least these memories remind me of what we use to have, and what we could have again. Every marriage has its rough patches, right?

Talk soon,
Michelle

May 20, 2016
Suzanne—a quick scribble to share that the new job is going great. Somehow each day is different and always interesting. I'm constantly learning. I think I'd underestimated the importance of structure, or how much better I do when I have

somewhere to be and goals to accomplish. The consistency of the workplace is such a relief after the endless drama elsewhere. I swear, a two-minute conversation at the coffee machine makes me feel like a new person! Maybe there's an element of escapism, too. My reality outside the office is not so wonderful right now, and putting my effort into a job where people appreciate my ideas and encourage my growth is amazing. It feels so good to be wanted! I have some heavy stuff to tell you but I can't, not yet. Sorry to leave you hanging. Don't worry, I'm fine. Just . . . not sure how to talk about it.

More to come (soon),

M

June 7, 2016

S,

Let's talk about me for a moment, shall we? Sorry, lame attempt at a joke. I guess it's time for me to fill you in. I know you won't judge me, but ugh. I've been dreading talking about it. Well, here goes.

For the last three months or so, since March, I've been self-harming.

There, I said it. It's out there in the world. With everything being so hard between me and Tracy, and with money still being tight, my heart and my head have been in turmoil. I want things to get better for Tracy and yet nothing I do works. I beg, I cry, I try to get him to open up, I threaten, I ignore. My attempts have made no difference, and they seem to only be turning him into a loner who doesn't want to engage with me, preferring instead to park himself on our white leather couch every day. There's a fine line between helping and micromanaging, and no matter what I do, I can't seem to get on the right side of it. He continues to spiral; our marriage continues to crumble.

We have not been on the same page for a single day since

we left Austin. What am I supposed to do? I don't know anymore, Suzanne. You know me—I'm a problem solver. Nine times out of ten I can look a challenge in the eye and get done what needs to get done. Not this time. I've never in my life been so frustrated. For a while, screaming for the fifteen-mile drive up the GA 400 on the way to work was enough of an outlet. I'd scream myself raspy, then take the Sidney Marcus exit, maybe stop by Starbucks to get something to soothe my throat, then be ready to face the day. If I needed to see a friendly face, I would visit my pal Tim Rice, an old Wilson college friend at his job at the Home Depot in the same strip mall as the Starbucks, get an affirming hug, and go on to the office. Or I'd hit the office kitchenette and either bask in the silence as I made myself a K-Cup or have a friendly chat with my co-workers before heading to my desk.

Turns out that the car screaming doesn't quite cut it. So I started hitting my legs at night, alone in the bedroom after the girls went to sleep. It wasn't premeditated or anything, like, *Hmm, I'm super frustrated, why don't I try hitting myself?* It just . . . happened. And it didn't feel good exactly, but it did feel different, which is at least better than bad. It hurts physically, but it's not anger or heartbreak or resignation or helplessness. Just pure, physical pain, pain delivered from the palm of my own hand. Pain and a sense of control.

In the morning, after that first time, I woke up with big purple bruises on my thighs. Was that a wake-up call? Nope. No one can see the bruises on my legs. In fact, no one can tell that there's anything going on. No one can look at my Facebook page and see what a mess my life has become. I can still be that actress walking down the red carpet to claim my award. Nothing to see here, folks; everything is A-OK! Only I know that it hurts to walk, that each step is torture.

One day recently, during yet another fight, I hit myself in anger. Tracy was screaming about something or other—who can remember at this point—with his fists clenched at his sides, and I was screaming back when the urge to pound on my thighs overwhelmed me. I'd been here before but had always managed to squelch the impulse. Not this time. Maybe it was a kind of a test, to see what would happen. Would it provoke Tracy? Would it scare him? Would it get me the tiniest bit of concern, even tenderness?

I hit my legs, as I'd been doing, but that didn't feel like enough, so I started pounding on the sides of my head. My brain was rattling around in there, and above the noise of my fists slamming my skull was the sound of Tracy's voice. "Michelle!" he yelled. "What are you doing?" I kept on hitting. "Michelle! Stop!" He came over and grabbed my hands, not aggressively but gently. This was the first soft touch we'd had in I don't know how long. "Michelle," he said, that tiny bit of concern I'd been craving clear in his voice. "Stop. You don't want to do that to yourself. Why don't you sit down and take a minute to relax. Michelle, this is not OK."

I wish I could say that was the end of it, but it's not. It's become my default coping mechanism when everything is spinning off axis. I know it's messed up. How stupid am I? What the hell am I doing? I have never done anything like this before. What kind of person hits herself? What if Justine and Charlotte saw me? What kind of example am I setting for them?

The worst was when we were at my mom's house. Tracy and I got into yet another argument, and I started to hit myself in front of her at her kitchen table. The girls were in the other room watching TV, thank goodness, and didn't have to witness Mommy going off the rails. But it shocked and scared my mom. I think for the most part she considers me pretty even keeled; I have never been the kid she has to worry too much about. (Mark has that dubious honor—what with his mental illness and occasional empty threats of violence, she worries about him a lot.) She'd never seen me so out of control.

Writing about this now, I'm completely embarrassed that I was "caught" by my mom. Perhaps the word I should use is "ashamed." I'm ashamed. Maybe it's a similar feeling to getting caught cheating on someone—you can't take it back, and you regret it, but it sure as hell felt good while it was happening.

Pooky, when will this stop? I don't know how much more of this crap I can take, to be honest with you. I just want to meet you down at Ginny's on a Thursday night for a couple of beers and do the two-step with some random guys before going home alone and happy. How do we get back to simpler times? I'm sorry to send you this letter. Call me and we can talk, OK?

Love you,

M

July 1, 2016

Pooky,

Justine turns two in a few days, and though she still isn't walking yet, she's made a ton of progress. Nowadays she's down to doing physical therapy once a week or so, and then she has her PT homework every day. Helping her is Tracy's full-time job and mission in life, and for that I'm eternally grateful. It's those moments when he's able to rally, to be the motivated Tracy I married, that I savor and stockpile in my mind for later, when things inevitably get tough again. They remind me that, no matter the state of our relationship, he's been a doting dad from day one. Remember when Charlotte was brand new, and he was adamant about taking her to our favorite local spots? No babysitters for our little girl—even though there's no way she would remember sitting on Tracy's lap at that restaurant with the dock at Lake Austin or going to SXSW for some great music and even better people watching—he was convinced that she would somehow absorb the good vibes. Tracy and sometimes Misty, his first wife, together with our baby, the two of them equally tatted up, her with a nose ring and awesome hair dyed jet black or blue or purple, depending on the month. Have you seen that photo where he's holding a beer in one hand and our baby girl, in a yellow onesie and hot-pink sound-canceling headphones, in the crook of his other arm? They were at SXSW. Charlotte was fast asleep and he's got this proud-papa grin on his face that makes me smile every time I think of it.

I rarely see that smile anymore, but I do get to see glimpses of that loving, patient side, which he reserves for the girls and, in particular, for Justine's physical therapy. I think her challenges make him love her even more—he's always rooted for (and probably related to) the underdog. Consistency is key, and he's her cheerleader and advocate and knows where to stop so she doesn't get stressed out or overtired. Our youngest is not what you'd call flexible—when she's done, she's done. Knowing that the girls are in good hands with him, that he's basically a different person around them than he is around me, allows me to go to work with no regrets. I do my job and earn the money during the day, and he takes care of them.

After work is something else. He'll "forget" to go to the grocery store, even on those days when it would have been easy enough to go after one of Justine's appointments, so I have to stop by on the way back from the office, and by the time I get home he's more than ready for a changing of the guards. It doesn't matter that I've been working my tail off all day and could really use a minute or two to myself. In that way, he's like Justine—when he's done, he's done. He'll stare daggers at me as soon as I walk in the door and, more often than not, I'll walk in to find the house an absolute disaster because instead of taking the girls out to the park or the library, he let them do whatever but didn't bother to clean up. Then I make dinner, do the dishes, and manage bath time and bedtime while he retires to the couch.

But he always gets Justine to her appointments on time. That's a lot, right?

Looking for that silver lining, dang it.

Love you,

M

July 29, 2016

S,

We haven't talked about sex in a while, have we? Not much to say, I guess. Sigh. For several years, we were like two bunny rabbits in the bedroom. So much intimacy and kissing all the time. There's been nothing since our anniversary on June 11, which was truly robotic, like checking a chore off the to-do list. Not make-up sex, not angry sex, certainly not regular couple-who-love-each-other sex. Nada. Full stop. And you know how it is in the summer, when everyone's half-naked and sweating, drinking icy lemonade with the condensation dripping down . . . you get the idea. I've been having hot flashes—oh, the joys of turning forty-three soon—and so I'm literally hot for so many reasons. Thoughts of other men have filled my fantasy world like you would not believe. Don't worry, it's all in my head. Still, it's making me crazy.

More than the lack of sex, though, is the lack of basic intimacy. Sometimes I'll simply walk in the door and if I look at Tracy the "wrong way," we'll get in an argument. It's like he holds it together for the girls all day, and by the time I get home there's nothing left for me. His drinking vodka and Gatorade all evening doesn't help. By the end of the night, he's an angry puddle on the couch, and once the girls go down for bed, I'm on my own. I sleep alone in our bed while he sleeps on the living room couch. I'm so lonely, Suzanne. And he is such a mess. Right now, he is downstairs, inconsolable, talking and mumbling to himself again. I wonder if his drinking is starting to become a problem. My God. I'm holding on, but barely. Once in a while, I need the old Tracy back.

We have two great kids. They are such smart, wonderful girls, and for them I have to keep a brave face. I know it's going to work out. . . . Don't worry. Maybe I've said too much this time. But it helps to get this out of my head. If I haven't told you how much our friendship means to me, I hope you can see that through these letters.

Love you always,

M

August 4, 2016

Hi, Suzanne,

Just dropping a quick line to let you know that I'm thinking of you. It's a typical August in Atlanta: hot, humid, and stormy. As I wrote last time, Justine is working hard on her physical therapy. She's learning how to train her brain to get her body to move in a way that, for most of us, is natural and expected. Hopefully our sweet little girl will surprise us all!

Love you,

M

August 8, 2016

S,

I found some cool stickers and thought of you. My kids are too young to appreciate them. Is your kid too old for these? Please pass them on with my love.

I'm feeling optimistic about the month as we have a few occasions to celebrate. OK, maybe it'll be a bit forced, but still! We celebrate my brother Mark's fifty-second birthday on the tenth and Tracy's forty-fifth on the seventeenth. We don't have anything planned except for some family dinners, but

I'm hoping these will pull them both out of the weird states they're in.

I think I've mentioned Mark and his ongoing battles with some pretty severe depression and mania. He was diagnosed as bipolar at some point, but I don't know if that's how he and his doctors talk about it now. Anyway, this summer he is definitely not doing well.

My dad recently dug up this essay Mark wrote in the 1980s, when we were living in Cagnes-sur-Mer, this gorgeous little seaside town on the Mediterranean. My dad had a sales job for IBM, and they were hiring English-speaking salespeople in Europe. We seriously lucked out when he got that gig based in Nice. White-pebbled beaches, blue skies, impossibly blue water. The best food in the world. Johnny was in high school and I was in middle school at the time, and Mark, who's nine years older than me, took a year off from college to join us overseas. I'm not sure where this essay is from—maybe a creative writing assignment? Anyway, it's short, so I'll just write it here:

> *About Me*
>
> *I'm just an average teenager with a lot of problems and hang-ups. I wasn't always like this, though, before I was an average preteen with problems and hang-ups.*
>
> *My name is Mark Vignault, and I am nineteen years old. That's hard to believe because when people look at me, they assume I'm fifteen when they see me.*
>
> *A lot that does to build my confidence.*
>
> *Some of the vices or traits that shape my personality are: paranoia, neurosis, enjoyment of staying in small dark places (what is this called), incisive neatness, martyrdom, laziness,*

and thinness (unable to eat enough). I could
probably go on indefinitely but for the sake of
being tied up I'll use the ones listed above.

Poor kid, right? He's always been a very sad person, like Pigpen with the cloud following behind him. I must have been pretty young, but I remember him cowering in the closet in the dark when we were kids. We didn't talk about it then. It was the 1970s in Georgia, not exactly the most say-what-you-feel era. This was before antidepressants, too, at least in our part of the world, and long before depression had lost its stigma, when it was considered a character flaw or moral failing. My parents were probably embarrassed or ashamed or hoping it was hormones and he'd just grow out of it. Or maybe they had no idea what they were looking at.

By the time I was eighteen, when he attempted suicide for the first time—or at least the first time I heard about—he was only twenty-seven. I remember knowing the word "depression" at that point. Was that a 1980s word? I had to look it up: Prozac hit the market in 1987, the same year as my first Duran Duran concert (on May 2 in Frejus, France, on their Strange Behaviour Tour). I think that's when wellness marketing really started to catch on, with Jane Fonda in those amazing high-cut leotards and leg warmers and the eye-candy handsomeness of David Hasselhoff, with that poofy hair and teeny tiny bathing suit. OK, I've gone down an internet rabbit hole here. It's easier to think about that than my brother's lifetime of mental health issues. Not much has changed over the last thirty years, and I honestly don't know how many suicide attempts he's had. This was part of why I moved to Austin and stayed there—it was too hard to deal with.

This past spring, Mark was on one of his manic upswings and, let me tell you, his highs are exceptionally high. He'll walk in the room already talking at full speed, and all you can do is ride the wave with him. You don't know how the conversation is going to curve and jump around. He could be talking full speed about a Martin Scorsese film, then a meal we had three decades ago, then where the girls are going for kindergarten, then on to some other completely random topic, followed by some other completely random topic, and so on. It's like a game of Ping-Pong, the way his thoughts bounce around. I don't know how he's held down a job at that French restaurant close to where my office is—thank goodness the owner is an old friend of his.

I'm not sure if this is better or worse than his lows. For me, I mean. Obviously, I wouldn't wish severe depression on anyone. After this latest manic episode, he went to a really dark place, hiding away, as he does, and not returning phone calls or texts. Then he had a breakdown a few weeks ago, in July. My dad does not always share the particulars, but he did tell us that Mark attempted to take his life. Again. He was in the hospital for seven days, with a sitter stationed outside his room. I was not allowed to see him. When he came out of the hospital, he was different. A light has dimmed and it doesn't seem to be turning back on. Now his conversations are short, not rude but like he doesn't have the energy to engage beyond the most basic level. His eyes are . . . distant, as though he's looking into some faraway place no one else can see. As if he was saving his energy for a marathon that only he will run.

This is the first time, as an adult, that I've lived close by and seen what his day-to-day life is like. I didn't quite get it before, hearing about it secondhand from my parents, but I do now. I'm worried about him.

Love ya, girl.

Michelle

August 13, 2016

S,

Mark hasn't been sleeping. At his birthday dinner at our house, he went back and forth between static dejection and agitation, pacing around the kitchen and touching everything and muttering to himself. Tracy, meanwhile, had been gulping his regular concoction of vodka and Gatorade, and he had that bright-red face and mean glare he gets toward his personal witching hour. I was sure that any minute sparks would start flying, so I put my arm around Mark's shoulders and guided him toward the door.

For a while I'd been mentally rehearsing a conversation, one that I've been dreading. There's just no way to broach the topic of murder-suicide or mass shootings delicately, is there? Because Mark has guns. Lots of people have guns around here, and whatever my opinions on the issue, it's not considered a big deal in Georgia. Besides when driving by the Sandy Springs Gun Range every day on the way to work, I don't pay much attention to it. Mark practices there but not to improve his hunting. He's really the last person who should have a gun collection since his mental illness comes with paranoia and grandiosity, which gets better or worse depending on his state. In his worse times, I think he truly believes that someone's out to get him. No idea who, or why they would care about a fifty-two-year-old dude with no important contacts and not much money. He has nothing worth stealing—to call his little condo a bachelor pad is being nice. (I doubt he's cleaned his bathroom since he moved in there.) He does love those Martin Scorsese and Tarantino movies and probably fantasizes about being the top dog at the big table in the Italian restaurant, with the gold chains and the hot young girls in tight cocktail dresses that he dismisses with a flick of the wrist when it's time for the guys to get down to business. If he could live in those movies, he would. He would admit as much.

My dad has tried to convince him to sell his guns many times and, when he refused, tried to take them away. He's even tried to break into Mark's house and steal them, all for his own good. My mom, meanwhile, is afraid of her own son, and it's been a long time since she's invited him over solo. I know in my heart that he wouldn't hurt a fly, but he's said weird things to her, like, "If I'm going to take anyone with me, I'd take you."

I'm scared he's headed toward another suicide attempt, and even more scared that he might do something crazy. Like I said, he's fifty-two, unmarried, no kids. He has nothing to lose. I've wondered many times over the past couple of months about these school shooters, or those guys (it's usually white men) who randomly gun down people at movie theaters or shoot into crowds at outdoor concerts. Can it really be that no one in their lives saw any signs of detachment from conscience, of impending violence? Or did they see signs but were just too afraid to bring them up? I would never ever forgive myself if Mark did something like that.

Outside the townhome, after the strange dinner held in his honor, I took a deep breath of the humid August air as I walked Mark to his car. He did that depressive shuffle, keeping his eyes down and barely lifting his feet off the sidewalk. It was now or never. "Mark," I said, "I wish you weren't going through this, and I hope you'll stick it out until you feel better." I paused, trying to find a way to break through to him. "Do you remember when you visited us in Austin right after Charlotte was born?" He looked at me, a good sign. "You were so sweet together," I continued. "You were so calm and loving, and she just relaxed in your arms. Uncle Marky. You remember?" He turned his face away. That would have to do. "I don't know why, but depression is your cross to bear. It's not your fault, it's no one's fault." I cleared my throat. The words were right there but, man, did I not want to say them.

"Please . . ." Another deep breath. He was looking in my general direction, just past me or over my shoulder. "If you are going to kill yourself, don't take anyone with you. Don't cause pain to strangers. Don't bring shame on our family." The slightest of nods. Then he got in his car and drove off.

I think, I hope, I pray, he heard me.

Love,

Michelle

August 29, 2016

Oh, Pooky.

Mark has been dating a woman his age (finally!), and he's been insisting for the last week that Mom and I bring the girls over for a Sunday dinner. This is unusual, especially given the depressed state he's in. But I was happy that he wanted us to get to know her and took it as a positive sign. Maybe they're getting serious. Her husband of thirty-plus years died about a year ago, and from the little I've gleaned, their marriage was a happy one. So even if *he* has no idea how to have a stable relationship, maybe she can show him the way.

Mom and I took the girls over to her house at around 2 p.m. yesterday. I'd told Mark that Tracy needed some alone time at home, when really he can't handle my brother when he's anxious. It was for the best—dealing with one unpredictable, moody man is enough for me.

Jan had a big, well-manicured home, with a tidy green lawn and a recent paint job; even her driveway was freshly power washed. Another positive sign: this is a woman who has her shit together. Pardon my French.

Mark was waiting at the garage door as I parked the minivan. I waved but avoided looking at him until I'd freed the girls from their car seats and slammed the passenger door shut. He was still standing there, in the same spot, with what I can only describe as a haunted aura surrounding him. He didn't look like he'd seen a ghost—he *was* the ghost. He was wearing his usual outfit, a polo shirt, khaki chino shorts, and big, ugly white sneakers on his outsize feet. His skin was beyond pale, as if all his blood had escaped him. "Hi, Mark," I said, giving his arm a gentle squeeze. He flinched as though I'd pinched him, then responded with a slight nod.

His girlfriend gave us a warm welcome. She was thrilled to have young children in her home, Jan told us, and the girls' joy in being in a new place to run around in broke up the tension. She seemed nice and sane, as well as age appropriate (at long last, Marky!), but let's just say that we didn't have much to talk about. After a basic tour, we ended up in her playroom, watching the girls play with some toys left over from her own kids, or maybe her grandkids. It was pleasant in an awkward kind of way that, with Mark, is more than I could've hoped for. I felt a little bit sorry for her—you could tell she was really trying, and he was not contributing one iota.

After an hour or so, we went downstairs for dinner. A simple meal with decent wine. Mark just sat there, picking at his food, moving it around on his plate like a little kid trying to avoid eating his brussels sprouts. Mark's a foodie, so that alone was weird, but I chalked it up to new meds or something else mental illness related. I couldn't quite reconcile the fact that he'd passed on wine, however. Mark never says no to wine. He's been working at Petite Violette forever and ever—that's where he and Jan met, she told us. Though he never got an official sommelier certification, the man knows his wine. The history, the terroir, the tannins, the minerality, and so on. When he's in a manic state, this is a topic we ardently avoid—get him started on it and he'll never stop.

There went my hope that a sip or two would loosen him up. He stayed completely self-contained for the entire forty-five minutes of dinner, and I was never in my life so grateful for the old parental excuse: *Well, we've had a lovely time, but we really should get the kids home for bedtime . . .*

As they walked us to the minivan, I got a strange feeling. Would this be the last time I'd see my oldest brother? Mark hadn't looked me in the eyes all afternoon. Hugging him good-bye was like hugging a mannequin. It's hard to describe. His body, his presence lacked . . . a soul.

In the car, my mom and I closed the doors and immediately looked at each other. We didn't say anything; we didn't have to. We both had the same fear in our eyes.

Love,

M

September 3, 2016

Suzanne,

On Tuesday morning, August 30, Mark killed himself. My dad called at 6:08 a.m., and I already knew what he was going to say when I saw his name on the caller ID. It wasn't a surprise, but still.

The story goes that Mark left his townhome, drove to Morgan Falls Park, and called the cops from his car to tell them what he was about to do. The park is at the end of a winding road, about three miles from the police station. In the time it took the police to get there, he went to the dock with one of his guns and shot himself in the chest. When they arrived, he was taking his final breaths.

I like to think that Mark went early so that no picnickers or little kids would find him. He chose a beautiful spot on the Chattahoochee River, where we often take—or took—the girls to feed the fish and ducks. I like to imagine that his last look at the world gave him peace, the trees filled with mist rising from the river, the sparrows singing, the water glassy calm. I hope that, even in his desperation, he was aware of the sun shining on his face.

He left a note in his car. It doesn't say much, but I'm glad he wrote it, at least to let us know he was thinking of us in his final moments. He wrote:

To Mom, Dad, John & Rowena, Michelle & Tracy, Sandy, Justine & Charlotte,

I can't take care of myself anymore. I can't sleep, and I can't focus. I'm just hurting my friends and family who care for me. I bequeath everything to my father, Walter Louis Vignault.

Mark L. Vignault

He was fifty-two years old. I don't blame him for his suicide. Does that sound strange? If you have been depressed for as long as he was, if you have been tormented by mental demons all your life, you run out of options. You get tired, tired of feeling bad, of trying and failing. He'd taken everything, Prozac, Wellbutrin, lithium, meds that worked for a minute and then stopped working. As far as I know, he'd decided a while ago that he was done. I'm pretty sure he was already gone by the time we saw him at his girlfriend's house for dinner. No more meds, no more therapy, no more check-ins with the psychiatrist. Depression is to blame for Mark's torment and, ultimately, his death. He didn't kill himself; depression killed him.

I'm comforted by the thought that my brother is now free from his pain. You are loved, Marky.

M

September 16, 2016

Suzanne,

The first part of this month was taken up by managing the logistics of Mark's death and the funeral. My being minutes away from my mom and dad rather than hundreds of miles means the world to me. I am so thankful to be here right now, girl. To be by Mom's side, making arrangements for my brother's cremation and church ceremony, and then hosting a party at our place (to show off the green carpet!) to celebrate Mark.

We had a memorial mass for him at St. Ann's on September 6. My mom's good friend Florence works there and helped us organize it. Johnny and his wife, Rowena, flew in from San Francisco, and a bunch of Mark's friends turned out to say goodbye. Two of my coworkers came—everyone at Clearion has been so supportive, so understanding. Even my good friend Matt, from the High Museum of Art docent program, came. His wife had taken her life years earlier, and so it meant the world to me that he was there, someone who knew what it was like to lose someone to mental illness.

The service passed in a blur. I remember saying something—someone from the family had to talk about how we loved Mark and would miss him—but I can't recall my exact words. After, the family and a small group drove the thirty minutes to the Arlington Memorial Park. My mom had already picked out her own niche in a mausoleum, but since her eldest son had died first, she'd decided to give it to him. I feel so bad for her. That's a hard pill to swallow for a mother.

There wasn't much to say and it was hot as hell, almost ninety degrees before noon. The quiet was pleasant, the only noise a babbling brook nearby; even the birds were off somewhere else, looking for shade. Just as the staff was about to close the little door in the mausoleum, Rowena lovingly slipped in a postcard with the Rolling Stones logo on it. A memento of Mark's favorite band, the band that provided him the soundtrack to his life, would keep my brother's remains company for the rest of forever.

A tree cracked in the woods in front of us, making a sound like a gunshot, then took its sweet time falling down, like the pause before a punchline. I think we all heard Mark in that moment, letting us know that he was OK. We had a good laugh.

After, we hosted a little gathering at our townhome. For a while, everything was fine. Good actually. Since Mark had never really left Atlanta, all of his people were here. Friends going back to high school and college, friends and their wives who had remained dedicated to him for decades. Johnny's old Atlanta buddies came out, too. It was so great to have so many creative and funny people in one place. Everyone was drinking and talking about Mark and the weird, quirky things he used to do, how when he was well or at least somewhat coherent, he could be so fun to be around. He was one of those guys who inspired love and loyalty, maybe in part because he was clearly so fragile.

Part of me couldn't help thinking, *Why didn't we have a gathering or something like this when he was here, when he was alive?* Maybe that would've been a lifeline. He would have had the best freaking time.

I'm familiar with these kinds of thoughts, these what-ifs. What if this, what if that. They are pointless.

Tracy was jovial for a while, enjoying the good wine and the party atmosphere. Up until his witching hour arrived. Then he got red-eyed and bitter, and I was distracted from what we'd all come here for. Pretty soon folks picked up on the vibe and scattered.

I cleaned up while Tracy retired to the groove his body had formed in the couch. As I gathered empty wine bottles and glasses with red stains on the bottoms, I thought about how good it would feel to go upstairs and hit myself. The relief, the release. But when the house was in a tidy enough state for me to call it a night, I found that I no longer had the urge. No idea why. Maybe because this hurt feels right—my brother killed himself, and so it's completely normal to be in pain. Or maybe it's because the helplessness of it is the helplessness inherent in death, rather than the helplessness of having a spouse who just doesn't seem to care anymore, at least not about me, and not about himself either. Whatever the reason, I went upstairs and fell into bed, no self-harm needed.

The next day, my dad asked me and Johnny to go through Mark's things at his condo. Rowena came along for moral support. Tracy stayed home with the girls. As he was a long-time bachelor, Mark's organization methods included stacking books and music on the floor instead of placing them tidily on the available shelves. Clothes lay piled on the bedroom floor, and may have been there for months. It's hard to say. The most interesting item, found by John, was a handwritten list of all the women Mark had sex with over the years. And what they did together—a little more info than I'd bargained for that day. Marky, as I liked to call him, had almost nothing worth saving. Just stacks of DVDs, mismatched dishware, some clothes that would fit no one, a couple of bottles of decent wine. Johnny took a few DVDs, even though the movies can all now be streamed, and some other loose pictures. I took a few books, titles he'd mentioned and that made me think of him, and a couple of framed photos. Johnny helped me gather up his albums, his beloved Rolling Stones posters, and a few other personal items to put into the back of our minivan.

At home, we walked in to find Tracy in a state. "Why are you back so soon?" was the first thing he asked.

Johnny and I looked at each other. "What do you mean?" I said.

"Why aren't you there helping your dad? You should be helping more!"

I took a deep breath. I could feel a blush coming on. Before the previous night, Johnny and Rowena had never witnessed Tracy in unreasonable-and-angry mode. "Tracy, we've done everything we need to do at the moment," I said softly, as though I were talking to a wild animal.

"You're not doing enough!"

That did it. I'd been holding myself together, but this was the final straw. Could I have just a droplet of compassion from my husband after the death of my brother, just a few minutes of support? "We're the ones who just lost a brother," I said through gritted teeth. "So what are you so damn angry about?" Clearly Tracy was itching for a fight, and I wasn't going to give it to him. I walked past him into the kitchen, where I poured myself a glass of water with shaking hands. In this full house, I felt an overwhelming sense of being alone. I recognized this feeling, this feeling of being married and alone. It's a different level of loneliness, blended with disappointment. Isn't one of the main promises of marriage that you won't have to be alone, that someone will always have your back when you need them?

Per usual, I stuffed my feelings down. I had other things to do, other matters to attend to, two little girls who'd be up from their naps soon and would want snacks and snuggles.

Life continues, of course, even as we grieve and plan and take care of business. In a way, focusing on the boring details gives me a break from the hard stuff. I'm happy to say that we are finally beginning to get back on our feet financially. I'm so proud of never having had to ask for financial support from our families through all of this. Yes, we've been down to a hundred dollars in our bank account and, yes, we've wiped out thousands of dollars in 401(k) savings. But we never asked for help, and that is a great feeling.

As fate would have it, this week the rental washer and dryer broke. At the same time. So what is the logical next step? Take the washer and dryer from your recently deceased brother's townhome. Lose a brother, gain appliances. Icky feelings. Sigh.

On top of that, we've managed to have our gas shut off. When you're dealing with the loss of a sibling, the mail and bills slip down the list of priorities. The process of turning it back on took a few days, so cold showers were in order. Compared to everything else, this is nothing, right? But, c'mon! September can stick it where the sun doesn't shine.

I listened to your voice mail. Thank you for wanting to be here for us, but there is so much going on right now, and I'd much rather save a visit for when things settle down, OK?

Lots and lots of love,
Michelle

October 3, 2016

Pooky,

October is one of my favorite months thanks to Halloween and your birthday. It's impossible to be sad when you've got two little girls dressed as a pumpkin and a sheep (last year's adorable costumes) and high on sugar. I've been bringing it up, just to see them get excited about it. It helps lift the grief fog. That, and knowing Mark is at peace. Not that I have time to actually grieve. I took a week off work, but there's just too much chaos for me to sit with my feelings or whatever it is we're supposed to do these days. When I get down, I try to remind myself that he's in a better place, hanging with David Bowie and all the rockers he looked up to. How is it that Mick Jagger and Keith Richards outlived him?

We've been friendly with some of the immediate neighbors and a few of them are from Paris—they are related and live a couple of doors apart. For a little while there I was getting the chance to dust off my French, but at some point, we managed to get on their shit list and they stopped liking us. Given, we've had a very busy home with many people coming and going, and they likely hear us yelling all the time. We've probably annoyed them, or they just think we're shady characters. I can see why. But still, did they have to complain to the HOA about our grass being too high? Seriously, our front yard is the size of a postage stamp. I got home the other day to find a citation stuck on our front door, and another argument with Tracy ensued, the cherry on top of the argument we'd just had about who had the time to cut the grass in the first place. Neither of us did, it didn't get done, and here we are, with another ticket to waste our precious money on. Merci beaucoup, neighbors.

At least this makes me more motivated for house hunting. Not only did we inherit Mark's washer and dryer, we inherited some of the proceeds from the sale of his condo, which we're planning to use for a down payment. I scroll through real estate porn whenever I have a minute, and Tracy sends me houses he's found online, too. When pitching our weekend open house trips to the girls, we've managed to frame them as a fun adventure. "How would you like new rooms?" we tell them. It's something to look forward to.

M

October 14, 2016
Suzanne,

I've been worried about Mackey for some time, especially since Luci died in April. She was his constant companion, and he has been depressed since her death. He has lost his desire for walks to the QT gas station down the road, and he is sleeping a lot. He's slowing down, girl. Tracy and I have been talking about what to do, whether to let him go or not. Like most things these days, we tend to disagree on what's the best choice for him. Even when it comes to our old dog, I can do nothing right in my husband's eyes.

Mackey has been my dog all these years, so I decided that, at the end of the day, the decision was mine. Tracy refused to go with me to the vet, but I reasoned that it also made sense for him to stay home with the girls. I thought I was strong enough to handle it by myself, but as soon as I got there, I lost it. I was full-on sobbing, sitting there with Mackey in the car, and so I called my mom. Bless her heart, she dropped everything and drove over as soon as she could, arriving about ten minutes later. While I was in the room with my dog, she sat waiting in the hallway. Just knowing that I wasn't alone made all the difference. My mom has always had my back.

After Mackey left this world, Mom went her way and I drove home, tears streaming down my face. My two dogs and my oldest brother, all gone within a year. I was met with little sympathy when I got home and grieved on my own, though I was able to go upstairs to the bedroom, to my king-size safe place, and actually nap for a few hours. Tracy must have told Charlotte and Justine to let me rest, and for that one small thing, I am grateful.

Aarf,

Michelle

October 20, 2016

S,

Since I've been too busy to go down the street to the communal mailboxes, I have just learned about my jury summons. I've already missed so much work recently, and I've come to rely on it as a respite from the parts of life that are weighing me down, from grief and my husband's anger. The last thing I wanted to do is take another day away from work to go serve on a jury. But it's my civic duty and all that, so I got up even earlier than usual to catch the bus near the old Atlanta Braves stadium, Turner Field, at 7:30 a.m. I could barely keep my eyes open for the twenty-minute ride to the downtown courthouse, and while waiting for my number to be called I had nothing else to do but sit there with my mind wandering to all the places I didn't want it to go: thoughts of my dead brother, my dead dogs, my dying marriage, the bills piling up . . .

There were fifty people in my group, and each of us was called one by one to go into another room to answer questions. Oh. My. Goodness. In the end I was not chosen (yay!), but by then it was 5:00 p.m., so after sitting in traffic to get back north, I made it home about the same time as I normally would. That was a long, long day.

Complaining done.

Happy birthday! Tomorrow is your big day. You are the best friend ever. I love you so much. I wish I was there to celebrate with you. What fun plans do you have?

Lots of love,

M

November 4, 2016
Hi Suzanne,

Can you believe how time flies? Charlotte turned four yesterday. Four! She's walking and talking like a little person because . . . she is one? It's amazing to me how they go from these tiny bundles of cuteness to full-on human beings with complex feelings and complicated needs and all that.

A week or so ago, we went to a pumpkin patch and picked out a pumpkin. At home, we carved it into a smiling three-toothed jack-o'-lantern and put it on the stoop of our town-home. On Halloween, we took the girls trick-or-treating in my dad and Sandy's neighborhood. I wore all black with a long, flowy purple wig. Tracy wore a black zippered onesie with cat ears, which made all of us laugh. One girl was a pumpkin, the other was a lamb. They were so cute in their little costumes, racing up the block and then back to us as we followed behind them at our slower grown-ups' pace. It's a small neighborhood with only thirty houses or so, but that was just perfect for them. The world is so big at that age.

Tracy put on his game face for door knocking, which a small part of me could recognize and appreciate while a much larger part of me resented it. I have to admit that my heart is pretty hardened at this point. He had no sympathy for me when my brother died, and he gave me a hard time when Mackey was so sick. He actually made my brother's death and Mackey's death harder! It's like a never-ending Me Show, with Tracy as the star. His feelings, his concerns, are the only ones that matter. And yet it's like he's also becoming this shell of a person, like he's retreating into himself. At least the big emotional outbursts are getting fewer and farther between (though when they do happen, watch out!). I hate to say this, let alone think it, but he's almost like how Mark was at the very end, when my brother was elsewhere even when he was standing right in front of me. Tracy has nothing to offer anyone, nothing for me except a wall that I no longer have the energy to bang my head against. I'm too tired to try to pull him out of this, to be introspective on his behalf. All I can do is get through the day.

Does that make me a terrible person? Well, too bad, I guess. I'm a terrible person.

Sorry not sorry,

M

November 6, 2016

Suzanne,

Another month, another start. Halloween with two little ones was so fun and a much-needed break from all the seriousness. There is a lot to look forward to. Johnny and Rowena will likely stay in California and spend the holidays with her side of the family, so it'll be up to me to plan something with Mom and Dad. Of us three kids, Mark was the one to always be close by and, whether he was high or low, the fact that he could be relied on to be in town was key. This will be the first Thanksgiving and Christmas without him. It's a lot for my parents to get used to.

In other news, the other day Tracy hopped in our minivan to go to the grocery store, but it wouldn't start. Ring, ring. "Hi, Mom, I need your help. Again." And so Mom came over and called AAA. It turned out that all we needed was a battery changed out and we were done! Except then the fix-it guy burned out the power steering and blamed us. It was $1,300 to fix, and he'd put us over a barrel. Mom saved the day. Again. Again, and again. Now we owe her a ton of money. Thank goodness this was our first financial ask. Thank goodness she remained calm for all of us. So many sighs.

Are we having fun yet?

Michelle

December 1, 2016

Dear Suzanne,

I hope you had a wonderful Thanksgiving. Before I get into it, let me just say that I am grateful for you. I'm grateful for my beautiful children. I am grateful for my fantastic job and amazing coworkers. I'm grateful for my mom and dad.

Notice anyone missing from the list?

This Thanksgiving was like none other. It was my dad's first without Mark. We went to his and Sandy's house for an early dinner. My brother always brought the wine, but since my dad and Sandy aren't big drinkers, this year we went without. I didn't much miss it, though I wouldn't have minded a little something to take the edge off. Fortunately, the girls were being extra cute, or so it seemed to me, which helped keep us from thinking about who wasn't sitting at the table. We stuffed ourselves with turkey, Stove Top stuffing, mashed potatoes and yams and green beans, and the girls plowed through a bag of King's Hawaiian sweet rolls. We left after a couple of hours with very full bellies to get the girls to bed at a normal hour.

A mostly mellow if somewhat sad holiday. It wasn't until Tracy's witching hour that an epic fight began. I poked the bear, Suzanne. I must have gotten a second (third, fourth, fortieth?) wind somewhere, and a sudden hopefulness replaced my apathy. I wanted to know what was going on. I wanted to talk as friends, dammit. Not even as husband and wife, or parents, or anything like that. I had no agenda, no ask. It didn't matter to me if he got a job or not, if he picked up the slack while I was at work. I wanted to get to the root of things, or at least start digging at the surface. I was just a person who cares about another person, despite the hostility and the self-pity and all the walls that person has put up. "What is going on?" I asked him. "What can I do? Why are things so bad?"

I just wanted a genuine conversation, I swear. This was poking the bear, because for a while I wouldn't take no for an answer. He, in turn, got mean. "What do you want? What do you want? What do you want?" he yelled. We were in our bedroom, in this small triangle of space between the end of the king-size bed, the big dark-wood dresser, and the bathroom. There was no room, nowhere to step back, and he, with a big puffed-out chest, was all up in my Hula-Hoop zone. Everything got too close again, like that late-night fight in the hotel room in New Orleans and too many fights since.

"That's it," I said. I was shaking, on the verge of tears. "I have to leave." He just laughed and said, "Fine, leave," then went downstairs to his couch.

I packed a small bag with my contact lens case and solution, my glasses, a toothbrush, my PJs, and my precious face cream, Noxzema, that was passed down from my mom. It was after midnight by the time I got outside and closed the door gently behind me. The streets were empty, with a few dried leaves blowing in the wind.

I drove around in circles for a while. I didn't want to call my mom or my dad and wake them up. I thought of my dear friends Sophia and Kelley, who lived just past Morgan Falls Park, but I didn't want to have to explain what was going on, why I had left my family so late on Thanksgiving. Finally, I drove over to the Perimeter Mall, where I remembered seeing several corporate hotels. I chose one at random, pulled into the parking lot, and dragged my sorry self inside.

I blinked in the sterile and entirely too bright lobby. For

a moment I felt dizzy, and I had this weird thought that the hotel was laughing at me. Like, *Ha, ha, you're alone tonight, your family is down the street but you're not there . . .*

A few minutes later, a clerk walked around a corner to greet me. His hair was tussled, like maybe he'd been sleeping, and he looked about as thrilled as I felt to be having a conversation at this hour. A clerk's job is to be welcoming and hospitable and all that, but not at 1:30 a.m. I hoped he was getting paid overtime. We hustled through the check-in process with no small talk and little eye contact, me gritting my teeth while he took my credit card and set up the room key. "Would you like to sign up for our reward program?" he asked as he handed it over across the counter. No, no, I did not.

The perfectly made bed in the spotless beige room of a generic, soulless, cookie-cutter hotel matched the way I felt about my husband and my marriage. Colorless and lonely and empty, with hospital corners that hid a nothingness underneath. All I could do was set the alarm on my phone and cry before dropping into sleep. I woke at 6:15 a.m. in the same position I'd fallen asleep in. I grabbed my stuff and got out of there, determined to get home before the girls woke up. I walked in just as they were popping out of their bedroom, hair in tangles and all excited to start the new day. Yippee. I made breakfast for three and a big steaming cup of coffee for one. Tracy was still asleep on the couch in the living room, but I didn't even try to be quiet.

Suzanne, I think I'm drowning. I know I keep saying that, and I keep meaning it, too. I'm drowning again, or more, or maybe in a new way. Why is it so hard right now? I know, there is no satisfying answer to the question. I do know that to be alone in a marriage, in this marriage, is far different and more difficult than being single and alone. There are different levels of loneliness.

I hope you don't mind me bringing you all this heavy stuff

right now. I have to remind myself that the holidays are hard for everyone. I love you. Thank you for everything,

M

December 14, 2016
Pooky,

Tracy has thrown in the towel as far as house hunting goes. Apparently, I don't have enough on my to-do list, so why not add housing to it?

Whining about it isn't going to change anything. If I want to move, then it's on me to figure it out. Light some incense and send good vibes from Austin for me.

Always,

M

December 22, 2016
Oh, Suzanne.

The holidays do not bring out the best in us, that's for sure. Tracy and I have reached another low point. (Is it even possible to go lower than we already are? It appears so.) We were fighting again about who knows or who cares what. It wasn't even all that late in the day, but Tracy was in a mood. I was in a mood too and had less than zero patience for whatever his issue was in that moment. We were at the top of the stairs, yelling into each other's faces, getting way too close. Again. We're on the brink of something bad, something really bad. Tracy's breath is hot on my face, and I can smell alcohol. I'm filled with rage, but I don't want to pound on my own legs—I want to pound on him. I want to hit him. I want to hurt him. Is this it? Are we going to tip over the edge this time?

Out of nowhere, Charlotte is standing there in the hallway on the bright-green carpet looking up at us with her big blue eyes. We stop in our tracks. Tracy takes a step back. I take a step back.

Later, as I'm tucking Charlotte into bed, she says, "If you leave, I'll go with you." My stomach dropped. In that moment, I had a flashback to a time when we were in France. I was ten or eleven. My bedroom was on the other side of the wall from the kitchen, and many nights I lay in bed and listened to my parents going at it. My dad and mom argued a lot, and there was other stuff, too. Once, when Mark was visiting, I heard him run down the hall to the kitchen. I got out of bed and peeked around the corner to see Mark trying to pull my dad off my mom. That put an end to it pretty quickly. It was awful. Sometime later, I told my mom, "If anything happens, I'll come with you, Mommy."

That's why I hated my dad for so long. We never talked about it, never talked about anything. As far as stuffing things down goes, the apple doesn't fall too far from the tree.

I never ever wanted this for my children. Back when Christian and I got divorced, I vowed that I would never do that again. If I ever got married again, I would stick it out. But something has to change. Once we move—did I mention we found a house?—I'll figure it out.

Love you,
M

December 30, 2016

OMG Suzanne!!!

You won't believe my good news. We had some money for Christmas gifts this year, but there could be no better gift than the one Justine gave us. Over the weekend, the four of us were hanging out in the living room, playing, and Tracy, Charlotte, and I were encouraging Justine to use her walker toy, same as usual. Using the couch, she pulled herself to standing, but for whatever reason, this time felt different. The three of us got quiet; the world slowed, like those slo-mo shots in sports movies, where the bases are loaded and the team is down three runs and it's the runty underdog's turn at bat.

Justine is standing there. Her walker is next to her, but she doesn't put her hand on it. We hold our breaths. She pauses, then takes a step. Unassisted. Then another. And another!

Remember that scene in *Rudy*, when the crowd chants his name and he sacks the quarterback in the final seconds of the game and his teammates carry him off the field? That's how it felt. Glory hallelujah! Juuuustine! Juuuustine! Juuuustine!

Charlotte cheered. Tracy and I cried like babies. She'd done it! At two and a half, our baby girl took her first steps. I'm crying right now, as I write this. It was one of the happiest, proudest moments of my life. It was everything.

I will always be thankful to Tracy, who encouraged her, worked with her, and loved her so much through this entire process. They did it! Our girl is walking!

Going into the new year with new hope. I wish I could hug you right now.

Off to find some tissues,

M

January 8, 2017

Pooky,

One look in the mirror reminds me that our college days are long gone. Thank goodness, though I did look good in a sweater vest if I do say so myself. It's been a long time, too, since I went through my little experimentation phase with hallucinogens, which are apparently all the rage now. As are mom jeans! We were ahead of our time.

Luckily, my limited, long-ago experience prepared me for last Wednesday and Thursday night. It was a typical morning on Hump Day, except that we're moving again. We've found a house halfway between my mom's house and my dad's. I feel like the valve on the pressure cooker that is our life has been opened just a sliver. It's not that Tracy and I are getting along better exactly or that, all of a sudden, he's turned into Mr. Cuddles. It's more like we have a shared focus that isn't tied to a particular resentment. As long as I don't think too hard about the fact that I'm the one who found the place, and that it'll be my income that's paying the mortgage. Or that my brother had to die for us to take this next step. Stuff it down, Michelle, stuff it down. We both wanted to move out of this townhome, and now we are. I sure WON'T miss the green carpet.

There's one weird thing I have to mention. I started packing as soon as the first contract was signed, and when I opened the closet door in the living room to get the girls' board games, I made a strange discovery. On top of the tattered Monopoly and Sorry! boxes, shoved in the back, were some empty vodka bottles. Eight full-size Tito's—good ol' Austin-made vodka. I didn't know what to make of it—I still don't—so I just tossed them in the recycling bin and mostly forgot about it. Obviously, the bottles are Tracy's, but why were they in the living room closet? And why so many? It's not worth bringing up, at least not right now. I cannot handle getting into it, what with everything that needs to happen in the coming weeks.

So anyway, a few days ago, I left our townhome packed wall to wall with boxes and headed out to work. I can't remember if I left the house with goodbyes and kisses, or silence and anger.

Fast forward to when I get home. Charlotte and Justine are still excited to see me after being away all day. A typical night of dinner, play, books, bath, and bedtime. I go to bed at around 10 p.m., per usual. Tracy was on the couch where I left him, per usual. Nothing exciting. Until the clock struck midnight.

I'm awakened by Tracy shaking me. He looks like he's tweaking: bulging eyes, disheveled hair, bright-red face. "Do you see them out there?" he asks, darting from our king-size bed to the window and pulling the blinds aside to look out into the wooded area behind our building.

I'm groggy. "Who?" I ask.

"The police."

"What?"

"The police! They're shining their lights on the house. I think they're here for me."

I'm so confused. I get out of bed, cross over to the window, and look outside. The sky is clear, with a nearly full moon. I scan the woods, squinting at the wall of pine trees that line the fence of the small backyard, looking for the lights. "Um," I say after a minute. "No one is out there, hunny. It's OK." I put a hand on Tracy's back. It's damp with sweat. "Just come to bed."

He shrugs me off. "Shhh! Do you hear that?"

I listen and hear nothing. "Hear what, hunny?"

"The front door," he whispers. "They're here."

For the next three hours, I did whatever I could think of to keep Tracy calm and quiet so as not to wake the girls, who were sleeping in their room one door away. I tried to convince him to get in bed, to let me give him a back rub, to close his eyes and, God willing, go to sleep. Sometimes he'd be close to relaxing, then he'd sit up, leap out of bed, and race downstairs to the front door. I'd trail after him. "No one's out there," I said over and over. "It's late, let's go back to bed." Eventually he'd let me take his hand and lead him upstairs, back to bed, only to start the process all over again.

At some point, we managed to fall asleep. Morning came all too soon. I peeled myself out of bed and spent the time in the shower debating what I should do. I could not miss any more work. But could I leave the girls with Tracy? I didn't understand what was happening. Had he been high last night? Or had he had some kind of psychotic break? I'd never seen him that way. In his most manic phases, my brother Mark seemed to unhinge from reality, and he too thought people were out to get him. Hence the gun collection. But I'd never seen a full-on episode up close.

After I was dressed, I checked on Tracy. He was sleeping soundly, and when I gently shook him awake, he seemed OK. Groggy but clear, with no signs of any lingering panic or paranoia.

Work was tough. I was beyond exhausted and worrying constantly about what was going on at home. I sent Tracy texts throughout the day, just to check in and make sure he was of sound mind. Mundane texts like, *How was Justine's PT? Are we out of milk? What do you want for dinner?* His responses were equally mundane.

I drove home to find a relatively sane house and went through the usual routine of dinner, play, books, bath, and bedtime. *Phew,* I thought. *Must've been a one-off.*

At midnight, Tracy shook me awake, and we did the same thing all over again. Literally the same thing, with him convinced someone was here to get him and me calming him down and trying to get him to go to sleep.

I was an absolute zombie on Friday but, per usual, I put on my best face and pretended that everything was just hunky-dory. By now, I'm quite good at that. When I had to cry, I'd go to the bathroom, then splash my eyes with cold water to keep the red away. I hope no one noticed. I love this job with hard-working folks who feel comfortable stopping by my private office for a chat. I love having healthy relationships that allow me to put aside the craziness at home.

Thankfully, those two episodes were it. So far. I feel like I am losing the little control that I have of our family. What is happening? I don't understand, and I am not equipped to know the right next steps. For him or us. I do know that this cannot continue much longer. I am about to break. I can only be the strong one for so long.

What in the fuck is going on?

M

January 26, 2017

Pooky,

What a crazy week. I seriously hope to find humor in this shit one day.

On Monday, we closed on our new house. Tracy didn't go with me since I was signing the paperwork; instead he stayed home with the girls. Dad went with me and met the previous owner of twenty-plus years, a nice older gentleman with a scraggly gray ponytail who took the time to tell me about building the gazebo to cover the hot tub years ago. "Now, Michelle," he said and leaned across the table. "You know why people have a hot tub, don't you?" Wink. Oh, Mr. Fox, you sassy one.

After closing, I went home to do some more last-minute packing. The next day, the movers arrived bright and early and filled the truck while I drove the girls over to my mom's house so they'd be out of the way for the day. Tracy and I stuffed our cars full of boxes, and once we could not squeeze in another single item, I said, "Meet you at the new house!" and drove off.

I made it there first. The movers showed up next. "You see Tracy?" I asked.

"Yeah, he was locking up when we left. Said he'd be right behind us."

No problem. He had the only key to the new place, but we could wait a minute or two. After thirty minutes and a few unanswered texts, I called him. He was frantic, nearly in tears. "I can't find the new house," he said. I could hear the sound of traffic in the background.

"It's OK," I said, trying to calm him down. "We've only been here a handful of times." Which was true. But also, we were in a familiar neighborhood, and the fact that he (a) couldn't find the house and (b) was so frazzled was upsetting. Was he drunk? High? Having a psychotic break? Whatever the reason, I needed to make sure he got off the road while in this condition. "How about you meet me at that gas station near Dad's house on the corner. You know the one I'm talking about, right?"

"Yes," he said, relief in his voice. "Yes, see you there."

I found him sitting in his packed-full car, his forehead resting on the steering wheel. It was clear that he was in no shape for moving. I called my mom. "Hi," I said. "I can't answer a lot of questions at the moment, but can Tracy come over there right now? I think he needs to take a nap."

A pause. "Has he been having a hard time sleeping lately?"

"Yeah, something like that." I hated lying by omission, but I did not have the time or energy to get into it.

"Well, sure then," she said. "Call me later?"

I sighed. "Yes, of course, but I really have no idea when. I'm sorry, Mom. But the movers are waiting for me, so . . ."

"Got it, sure."

I hung up the phone. "Tracy?" I said. He lifted his head and looked at me, a confused expression on his face. His eyes were red rimmed and his forehead was sweaty. "Why don't you head on over to my mom's house?" He nodded. "You know how to get there?" He nodded again. "You sure?" Another nod. "Call me if you need me, OK?"

My mom texted me to let me know that he'd safely arrived and gone upstairs to her extra bedroom. With the key I returned to our new house, where the movers had been sitting around waiting on me. I apologized, knowing that I'd be doling out an extra big tip at the end of the day. I directed them and unloaded box after box after box, impressed with how fast we were able to work. We had a lot of time to make up for.

At 4:15 p.m. I decided that Mom had had the girls long enough, so I swung by her place to pick them up. Tracy was still sleeping. We needed to be completely out of the rental by 6:00 p.m., and rather than deal with getting him up and out, I bundled the girls into their winter coats and hustled out to the minivan, promising something yummy for dinner. At the townhome, I told them I'd be right back and rushed up to the door. There was a strange sound coming from the inside, a sort of *whoosh whoosh whoosh.*

What is that sound? I wondered. I unlocked the front door, and what did I see? Water falling from the ceiling into the dining room. I ran upstairs. Water was gushing out of the washer and dryer knobs. Chaos. Motherf——er!

I stood there in the doorway catching my breath, then called the landlord's fix-it guy as I rushed down the stairs to get the girls out of the car. It was getting dark, and there were two hungry girls ready for dinner. They're only two-and-a-half and four years old, mind you!

The fix-it guy, Justin, showed up fast, thank goodness, and was able to get the water to stop without too much trouble. I gathered up the very last odds and ends and hustled the girls back out to the car. They were whining at this point, and I didn't blame them. I felt like whining, too.

Chicken nuggets and fries at McDonald's was all it took to make them happy, and I thanked my lucky stars. Simple needs and simple pleasures on one hell of a day.

The three of us walked into our new house for the first time without Tracy. I had to stop for a moment and collect myself. I felt disoriented, nearly dizzy, with a sense of déjà vu. A few days ago, I'd had this weird dream in which Charlotte, Justine, and I were dancing in the house, just the three of us, and then playing outside on a warm, sunny day. I shook my head to rid myself of it, then ushered them in and up to their new bedrooms.

He's still asleep, Mom texted me when I asked. She'd been peeking in on him every now and then and he was snoring away, dead to the world.

I managed to get the girls' rooms situated enough for them

to pass out at 8 p.m. Tracy arrived at 11 p.m. He'd slept for nine hours. Nine. Hours. On moving day. What the eff? I was ready to pass out and he was fully rested, with grand plans to hook up the TV.

I can't even remember falling asleep.

In the morning, I woke to my gorgeous girls' happy faces. After a tough day, we're all so happy to be in our own house.

WTF.

Love,

M

February 4, 2017

Pooky,

I have so much to tell you.

The past week has been spent unpacking, working, unpacking more, working, unpacking more. The girls are settling in just fine. Charlotte in particular is thrilled to have her own bedroom. Now her sister can't steal her toys so easily.

Today has been one of the craziest days in a crazy week. First thing, I overhear Tracy downstairs, talking to himself. *Maybe he's on the phone,* I tell myself. *Maybe I'm dreaming.* Who am I kidding? He's been talking to himself, or rather, to Mark, these past few days. Once I heard him say, "Is it going to be OK, Mark?"

I sneak a look over the wall along the stairs to confirm. Yup, no one is there but him. It was really, really unsettling.

I didn't have time to dwell since Charlotte had her first soccer lesson with her "boyfriend," Thomas, this morning. Remember Tim and Tanairis and their kids, our very first Atlanta friends? Over the past year, we've spent a lot of time together, meeting for playground playdates and eating pizza at one another's houses, driving north to go apple picking, soccer. Did I mention that Tim and Tanairis are two of the few friends here who've met Tracy? Probably because he was willing to go places and do things when we first moved here, unlike now, when all he wants to do is stay home and watch TV or whatever it is he does. My coworkers haven't even met him. When they've asked about him in the past, I've always given some lame excuse like, "He's a financial analyst and very busy." Lies, of course. Anyway, this past fall, Charlotte and Thomas fell in love with their coach Carly, and so we went in together to hire her for private lessons through the winter.

So while the two older kids were off kicking the ball with Carly, and Tanairis was chasing Savannah and Justine, Tim and I caught up.

"Where's Tracy this morning?" Tim asked.

"He stayed home," I said. I paused and took a sip of my coffee. The gray clouds above seemed to drop a little lower in the sky. This most casual of questions did not have the most casual of answers, and a familiar part of me, the part that stuffs things down and puts on a happy face, wanted to change the subject. But something made me pause. A feeling in my gut or in my heart, a feeling that there was a momentum gathering, pushing me forward. "He, uh, he wasn't feeling too well," I added. I could feel Tim's gaze on me, but I kept my eyes on the field, pretending to focus on Charlotte and Thomas as they raced toward the goal. After a minute, Tim cleared his throat.

"You seem like you have something heavy on your mind," he said.

"Do I?" So cool, so casual. "Yeah, I guess I do. I don't know exactly how to say it, but I feel like something big is about to happen with our family. Does that sound crazy? I don't know what it is yet."

"You mean, with the move and everything?"

"That's part of it. But I'm actually thinking . . ." Deep breath. "I think Tracy has a drinking problem." This was the first time I'd said it out loud or, really, put it together so clearly in my own mind. I closed my eyes for a second, then looked at Tim to gauge his reaction.

"Oh," he said, clearly surprised. "I had no idea."

"Yeah, I'm kind of just realizing it myself. Ever since we moved here, things have been different. He's been different. He hasn't been doing well. And then when I was packing up our house last month, I found eight empty vodka bottles in the living room closet, next to the board games."

Tim exhaled and shook his head. "Yeah," he said, "not a good sign."

"I feel stupid, honestly. I mean, at first, I thought he was having a hard time because he missed Texas and then he hadn't found a job. He sort of seemed like my brother Mark did in his low times. Which was worrisome, of course, but somehow Tracy's always been able to show up for the girls, so I assumed that he was depressed but he'd snap out of it eventually. I mean, if he could hold it together for them, that meant he could still hold it together, right?"

"Makes sense," Tim said. "I'm not an expert or anything, but if someone is set on hiding it, then alcoholism can look a lot like straight depression."

"And I didn't know what I was looking at. I know mental illness, not addiction." I paused, mulling this over. Had I really not been able to tell the difference? Maybe, maybe not. But I had other things going on, a lot of other things, and Tracy had worked so hard to push me away. Maybe that's what he'd been going for. "Or," I added, "I was too busy to look closely." Another puzzle piece fell into place. "I think I'm going to have an intervention with Tracy when we get home," I whispered. I don't know where that came from—it was like divine inspiration, completely out of the blue. Another way to say that is it was completely unplanned and unresearched. I had no idea what goes into an intervention, only that it felt right.

"Wow, OK," Tim said. "Is there anything we can do to help?"

I checked the time on my phone. "How about pizza?" I said. "I'm not ready to go home yet."

After the lesson, we caravanned to a nearby fast-food pizza place. I was in a daze. I remember ordering some pizza for the girls, but that's about it. I can't remember what I ate, only that my body felt numb and wired at the same time. I couldn't bear to sit still, so I hovered over the girls, getting them water re-fills and napkins they didn't need, wiping their faces until they whined. Helicopter mom on overdrive. Anything to stay busy, to not have to think about next steps.

As we walked out to our cars, Tim asked gently, "Are you OK?" I shook my head. We'd filled Tanairis in on the basics at lunch, and now she stopped and took my hand. "Call us if you need anything," she said, then pulled me in for a hug. "Anything, you got it? We're here to help."

Tears welled up in my eyes. I nodded.

With the girls buckled into their car seats, I took a mo-ment to collect myself in the driver's seat and call my cham-pion. "Mom?" I said, trying to keep my voice steady. "Can you meet me at the house? I . . . I think I want to do an intervention with Tracy. And I don't think I can do it alone."

She was waiting for me when I pulled into the driveway. I waved, and she tentatively waved back, a look of concern on her face. As soon as I got out of the minivan, she came over. "What's going on?" she said in a soft voice.

"I've been having this weird feeling," I said in an equally soft voice, with a glance at the girls, who were off in little-kid day-dreams in their car seats. "I didn't know what it meant until this morning." I took a deep breath. "I think Tracy's drinking has in-creased. I found eight bottles of vodka hidden in the living room closet when I was packing. His agitation is getting worse, and he's talking to himself more, too. And then there are the hallu-cinations I told you about. This is nuts. I have to do something."

Mom nodded, unfazed.

"Would you mind taking the girls inside so I can call a few of Tracy's friends?"

Mom nodded again, then went around to the other side of the minivan. "My girls!" she said in her cheeriest voice, sliding open the passenger door, while I pulled up Marcelo in my contacts. He and Tracy have been besties since junior high, with a shared love of skateboarding and beer, and he just so happens to be a nurse. He's worked in the emergency room and has seen a lot of hard stuff, and he's about as solid a friend as you could imagine. Unlike my mom, he did not sound surprised, though he hadn't realized that things had gotten so bad. "We started drinking at fifteen," he said, "and Tracy never stopped. I told him that you can't party like you're in college your whole life." He got quiet for a second. "I'm glad he's going to get the help he needs."

Next, I called another one of his best buddies, Jose—also in the medical field—and gave him the news. Recently he'd talked to Tracy, who had told him about his two nights hiding from the imaginary police, and so already Jose knew that things were slipping. Although he'd been somewhat prepared for it, news of the intervention still came as a shock. He thought of Tracy as being so together, the guy with the great job, the guy who could ride a hundred miles on his bike, then meet up for drinks and dinner. In fact, a decade earlier, Tracy had offered him a place to stay at very low rent while Jose was trying to get on his feet and figure out what the heck he wanted to do with his life. He gives Tracy a chunk of credit for his successful career and for motivating him to follow his heart, to get married and have three beautiful children.

Finally, I talked to Tracy's ex-wife and our good friend, Misty. She and Tracy had been married for eighteen years, and I knew that they'd had a tumultuous relationship but were also best friends. For two seconds, I thought about asking her what his drinking had been like during their marriage but thought better of it. We'd never traded Tracy stories, and that was probably for the best. She did sound surprised, however, when I gave her a very condensed version of what was going on. She, along with Marcelo and Jose, agreed to be on standby for the rest of the day.

I hung up, feeling more resolute with the knowledge that these three people whom Tracy trusted would be there if I needed them. Inside, the house was as we'd left it, with boxes everywhere and framed pictures leaning against walls. My first instinct was to listen for the dogs' footsteps and jangling collars; my heart still sinks every time I'm met with silence and remember that Luci and Mackey are gone.

I could hear my mom and the girls upstairs and followed the sound. "I got this," I said to Mom as I entered the bath-room, where they were washing their hands and wiping dirt and tomato sauce from their faces. She nodded and I contin-ued with our naptime routine. Shoes off, blinds down, last-minute requests for water. Fortunately, Charlotte and Justine were tuckered out from soccer and playing with Savannah, and their bellies were full of pizza, so they went down for a nap without too much fuss.

I crept downstairs. Mom and Tracy were chatting in the family room, over the sound of pundits making predictions about the upcoming Super Bowl. He's come to rely on her, too, and he usually keeps his cool around her. They sounded happy, like it's just a regular visit, which I'm sure Tracy still thought it was. The cat was not yet out of the bag.

He was stationed in his usual spot on our white leather couch, his tall green cup filled with ice and orange Gatorade. Presumably Tito's vodka, too. Mom was sitting on the recliner, and I took a seat on the armrest next to her.

"Hi, hunny," I said.

He looked back and forth between the two of us. This

taking a seat was a departure from the norm for us—usually I'd be whirlwinding, clearing dishes from the kitchen table or starting a load of laundry or doing anything to get the chaos wrapped up. "Hi?" he said, a question in his voice.

"I think it's time we talked about your drinking." His eyebrows went up but he didn't say anything. I continued. "It seems like you've been drinking more lately, and I'm worried about you. We're worried about you." My mom nodded in agreement.

Tracy smiled the kind of smile you give when someone is being an idiot but you're willing to humor them for a minute. "Oh, really?" he said.

I looked at his recently freshened drink. "It's barely three in the afternoon," I said. "How many drinks have you had today?"

He rolled his eyes. *It's Saturday* was the implication, *and you were out with the girls.*

I took a deep breath, fortifying myself for what I'd known would be a less-than-productive conversation. We talked *at* him for the next hour or so while he leaned back on the couch, cool as a cucumber, barely listening. There was no yelling, no screaming, no tears. Just a full-on brush-off. "I don't know what you're talking about," he'd say, or "I really don't drink that much" or "You're overreacting."

Even though I had done just about zero research, I knew these were common responses, but it was out-of-this-world frustrating. By this point, I'd had it. I'd spent all morning on edge, my brain trying to comprehend what my next step was going to be. I was tired of not having answers, and physically, I didn't know how much more of this I could handle alone. Pardon my French, but it was time to shit or get off the pot. Stuffing down a problem was one thing; outright lying about it when confronted was another. I stepped out of the room and called 911. An odd choice, I realize looking back, but I figured that, if he wasn't going to listen to me and my mom, then I needed to do something drastic.

"911," said the voice on the phone. "What's your emergency?"

I told the dispatcher that my husband had a drinking problem and my mother and I were trying to have an intervention
but it wasn't going well. There were two little girls napping upstairs. Could they send someone to talk to him?

"Is he getting agitated or aggressive?"

"Not yet."

"Are you afraid that the situation could escalate? That
there could be violence?"

I thought about our last big fight at the top of the stairs,
when Charlotte arrived in the nick of time. "Yes," I said.

"We'll send someone right away. Would you prefer a silent
arrival?"

"Yes," I said, breathing a sigh of relief. No sirens to disturb
our new neighbors. "Thank you."

Thirty minutes later, an entourage of police officers, EMTs,
and firefighters were standing awkwardly in the living room.
Thank you, Cobb County! Tracy actually sat up at their arrival,
the embodiment of shock. It's amazing what a badge and a
uniform can do. "What the hell?" he said.

"They're here for your intervention," I told him. "Please,
will you just listen to them?"

One of the EMTs administered a wellness check, running through a checklist on her tablet. Was he having trouble
breathing? No. Was he disoriented or confused? No. What was
the day of the week? Saturday. Was he in pain? Yes, back pain,
but it was a chronic issue, not an emergency. Tracy stayed
calm, answering her questions about his medical history, his
allergies, the medications he was currently taking. He admitted that he drank too much vodka. That, at least, was progress,
but since he wasn't being physically aggressive or disruptive,
there was really nothing further they could do. After about
forty-five minutes, the first responders poured out of the house

as smoothly as they'd poured in. "Good luck," said one of the officers to me as he stepped out the front door.

We'd been here for eight days, and the neighbors must have been thinking crazy stuff about us already. Even with the silent arrival, I'm sure they noticed a police SUV, a fire truck, and an ambulance parked at the curb. Oh, well, who gives a fuck right now?

The girls woke up from their naps—thank goodness they both went down and stayed down from about 2:30 to 4:30, a rare stroke of luck on this Saturday. Mom and I took turns with them, as Tracy talked to Jose, Marcelo, and Misty in turn over the next few hours. I came and went, wanting to give him privacy but also curious as to whether they were getting through to him. By the time he hung up, he looked ragged, bone tired. "Fine," he said in my direction though without looking at me. "I'll go to rehab." Hallelujah. "But," he added, before I could get too excited, "not till Monday. Tomorrow is the Super Bowl."

I agreed. To Tracy, this is the holiest day of the year, and I knew trying to negotiate about it would be futile. This could be his one last hurrah, a sacred holiday before he takes a big, scary step. It's going to be hard for me to wait.

The rest of the evening was eerily quiet. Mom finally left at 10 p.m. My hero, as always. I could only trust that he wouldn't change his mind between then and Monday morning.

Here's hoping,

M

February 5, 2017

Pooky,

It's Super Bowl Sunday, a sacred holiday in the Fink household.

This morning was subdued. I'm pretty sure the girls aren't aware of what's going on, or at least they are distracted by the joy of claiming their rooms, getting out their toys, and organizing them to their own tastes. I, meanwhile, did some more much-needed unpacking and avoiding of my husband. To me he's like a sleeping lion—I tiptoe tiptoe tiptoe so as not to wake him. Even so, I'm feeling more at ease than I have in a while, knowing that there's a next step ahead of us, an actual action item I'll be able to check off my to-do list. All I wanted was for him to enjoy this day, to give him nothing that would make him change his mind about tomorrow.

It was late morning by the time the girls got hungry and came around for lunch. Tracy stuck to his couch, enthralled by the football fortune tellers and sparkly commercials. He had his usual Big Gulp cup, but I didn't see him refilling it or even drinking from it all that much. Then again, I hadn't seen him doing so in the last two years, so maybe my powers of observation could use a tune-up. After lunch, we let him be and headed out to the nearby playground, where we spent the afternoon climbing on the jungle gym and running through the grass, then returned home to order a couple of pizzas. By the time the game started, I was already on bath and bedtime duty, and I mostly stayed busy puttering about, hearing Tracy shouting at the TV every now and then. An uneventful day that, given the circumstances, is more than I could have hoped for. Wish me luck tomorrow.

Biting my nails over here,
M

February 6, 2017
Suzanne,

Tracy gulped down a glassful of vodka and Gatorade at 7:45 a.m. This was a first, at least for me. I'd never seen him drink so much at one time, or so early in the morning. Was this unusual for him, too, or was it something he did on the regular, once I leave the house for work? I'll ask him eventually, though not today.

As planned, Mom arrived at 8:00 a.m. on the dot. Of the many lessons she taught me, the importance of punctuality is at the top of the list. She shows up when she says she's going to show up, which is one less thing to worry about. I'd already called in sick to work and told the girls that they were getting to have a special day with Nana.

I watched nervously as Tracy said goodbye and hugged his daughters. Would he come along as he'd promised, or would he change his mind at the last second? Would he be cool about it, or would he be angry and harsh?

We got into the car, our seat belts clicking into their buckles the only sound. So far, so good. I turned the key in the ignition, put the gear into reverse, and looked over my right shoulder, to make sure my husband was situated in the passenger seat next to me. I could not believe what I saw. "Hunny?" I said. "Look at me again."

"Why?" he said, turning to face me more directly.

"I have never seen your eyes so . . . yellow. It's like they're glowing!"

Tracy flipped down the sun visor and examined himself in the mirror. "Huh," he said.

We arrived at Peachford Hospital at 8:30 a.m. and were handed a pen, a clipboard, and a stack of paperwork. We took a seat in the waiting room, alongside other incoming patients in various states of unkemptness filling out their own intake forms. Tracy wasn't up to filling out the forms himself, so I went through them, signing off on the legalese and asking him the standard intake questions. What had brought him here? What was his living situation? What was his history with alcohol and drugs? Date of last use? Other diagnosed medical conditions? Allergies? Medications? Seizures? When using, how much does he use? Any pending legal concerns? Detox history? Prior treatment? What was his motivation for seeking treatment?

Had I been awaiting some big epiphany, some golden nugget of information that would make the situation make sense? Maybe I was hoping he'd say, "Oh, I'm here to get better. I've been drinking since I was fifteen and successfully hiding it from the people I love, including my beloved wife, who has really borne the brunt of my addiction and its associated problematic behaviors. More than anything, I want to be the man she married, to fix our marriage, and to raise our beautiful children together in peace and harmony." On that front, I was to be disappointed. He was too disoriented to give much detail; there was a certain kind of blankness to him that I hadn't seen before.

At 11:00 a.m. or so, we followed a big, tall male nurse down a long hallway to a small exam room, where we waited until 1 p.m. as the caseworker came in and out, administering different tests and asking questions. Tracy participated each step of the way, but as the day went on and without even a snack to keep hunger at bay, he started to get aggravated. Squirming. Fidgeting. Restless. Vocal about the delay, the boredom, the slowness of the process. Maybe he was craving a drink; I didn't ask. Instead, I focused on keeping him calm. Could he just get up and leave at this point? I prayed that he wouldn't.

I was anxious too and kept looking at the clock, all too aware that the longer I stayed, the less time I had to tackle the next big thing: finding day care for the girls. To begin tomorrow. As generous as my mom is, I wouldn't ask her to take the kids all day, every day. That would be way, way too much. Obviously, I'd be the sole earner for the foreseeable future—those stay-at-home-mom dreams were but a very distant memory. So day care it is.

I avoided thinking about what I was going to tell Charlotte and Justine when they asked me where Daddy was.

Once the nurses were finally ready for me to leave, all of a sudden, I was hesitant. When would I get to see my husband next? How long would he be here for? Could I talk to him at the end of the day?

I knew none of the answers, but I had to go. I recall looking at him and feeling incredibly disconnected. Yet I kissed him. "I'm proud of you," I said. "Thank you for choosing to be here. We all love you." I squeezed his hand. "I'll talk to you soon." I walked out of that small, cold room, down the long, bright hallway, past the reception area packed with patients and the people who loved them. I didn't look back. My mind was already focused on the future. I imagined a new Tracy or, rather, the Tracy I'd fallen in love with, walking this same path to the exit, my meeting him outside. His eyes would be clear and bright, his gait would be steady. The bloat we'd never talked about, the big belly and puffy face, would be gone, a new glow of health like an aura around him. He'd smile that smile I hadn't seen in so long and open his arms to me. We'd both know that the road ahead was going to be long, that recovery is never one and done, but we would travel it together. I had hope. He was and always would be my daughters' father. We'd be a family again when he was ready.

My mom, the girls, and I spent the rest of the remaining hours before closing time driving around the neighborhood to check out day cares. I needed to be at the office tomorrow, so we didn't have the luxury of being too picky. Fortunately, we found one that can take them. It's not ideal, but it'll work for now. We got home a bit after 5 p.m., tired and satisfied and ready for dinner. Just as we were sitting down at the kitchen table, the phone rang. It was 6:08 p.m.

"We're so sorry," said a nurse from Peachford, "but your husband had a fall. He's on his way to Northside Hospital emergency room."

This is scary, Suzanne.

Talk when I can,

Michelle

PART THREE

WHAT HAPPENS TOMORROW

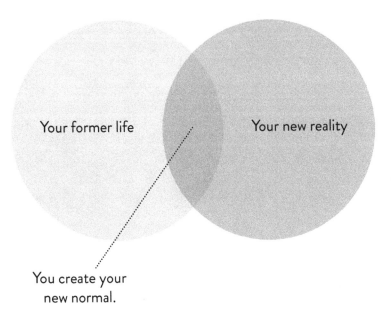

Your former life

Your new reality

You create your
new normal.

My own personal Venn diagram. Image © Michelle Vignault

February 6: Admitted. Jaundice & unconscious.

When it comes to emergencies, I'm your go-to gal. I can put aside my own panic or fear—it'll be there waiting for me to deal with later—and get down to business.

And so I was calm as I walked through the big sliding glass doors at Northside Hospital. I hadn't had to say anything to my mom when I hung up the phone. "Go," she'd said, nodding toward the door. As I'd grabbed my purse and keys, I overheard her saying in that chipper Nana voice, "Let's get ready for baths and bed!"

I approached the ER front desk and went into Southern politeness autopilot, taking the time to say hello and smile at the receptionist before asking about my husband. She clicked around on her computer, then pointed me toward a hallway. "You'll need to check in with the security department first," she said.

I said thank you and walked down the hall, where I found a little kiosk with a Dutch door, the kind with a split in the middle so that you can open the top half while keeping the bottom half closed. At my approach, a burly man in a nondescript navy-blue shirt stood up from behind a desk with a computer and security monitors. "Patient name?" he said.

"Tracy Fink."

He opened a big binder and looked at the front page. "He's

Once I'd been cleared, the security guard opened the bottom half of the door and came out to escort me down another long, wide hallway to Tracy's room—ICU room 6. I said thank you and walked in, briefly registering that it was unexpectedly nice, with a private bathroom and seating area. A figure lay on his back in the bed, a thin beige blanket pulled up and tucked in. "Tracy?" I said, not wanting to startle him. I needn't have bothered; he was completely out. Wires connected him to various monitors at the head of the bed, the only sound our breathing and the electronic beeps of medical equipment.

I was having difficulty processing what I was seeing. It was still Monday, the day after the Super Bowl, though it felt like a year had gone by. My husband had checked into rehab as promised. He'd submitted himself to the process, answering questions and allowing the nurses to take his vitals and do other nursing things. Just a few hours earlier, I'd left with hope in my heart, a happy feeling I'd missed. He'd get better, we'd get better, our home life would return to what it had been before the move. Before, apparently, his drinking had truly begun.

But instead of settling in and getting down to the hard work of facing his addiction, Tracy was here, in the ICU. How did this happen? All I was told was that he'd fallen, and I wondered if, after I left Peachford Hospital, he'd gotten agitated. Maybe there'd been a scuffle. I imagined a nurse calling for backup as one and then two orderlies restrained him, my husband ending up sweaty and red-faced on the ground, while another nurse ran up, prepping a syringe with sedative.

That fleeting thought about what had happened was all I had the time or energy for. I was more concerned with the here and now, the fact that my husband was lying unconscious in the ICU. I leaned over him, placing my hand on the bed next to his arm. "I'm here, hunny," I said. "You had a fall but they're taking care of you." It had been a while since I'd looked at him up close. He was puffy, bloated beyond belief, his stomach a hard orb beneath the blanket even in this horizontal position. He'd always had the fair skin tone of a redhead, but there was an inflamed pinkness to it now. His hair was lank and faded, nearly colorless. He looked awful.

Had he been like this before and I hadn't noticed? Or was this a recent development? The answer, if I were to be honest, was neither. His appearance had been deteriorating for a while, and I had noticed but written it off as another side effect of the depression. Once he got up off the couch, I'd decided, maybe got back on his bike or started running again, got a little sunshine on his skin, he'd be the handsome, fit Tracy of Austin, Texas. I had always held on to a sliver of faith that this would turn around eventually. I still believed.

After some time, a nurse with teal scrubs and a bouncy ponytail walked in. I provided basic information in a daze, mentioned his glowing yellow eyes. "Yes," she said. "He has jaundice. Alcohol related. We're going to keep him here until we can get him stabilized."

"Will he be able to return to rehab?" I asked.

"We need to run additional tests, and we'll know more in a couple of days. There are boxes we'll have to check before we can start thinking about that, OK?"

I nodded. I'd had enough thinking for the day. The nurse gave me a sympathetic smile. "Go home and get some sleep," she said. "There's nothing you can do for your husband right now. We'll take good care of him, I promise."

"Thank you." I checked my phone. It was getting late, and my mom had been on duty since eight o'clock that morning. My feet felt like two blocks of cement as I dragged myself back down the wide, long hallway, past the security kiosk, and out the sliding glass doors. Outside, a cool breeze blew across the parking lot, a nearly full moon shining above the glare of the security lights. A memory of another parking lot crossed my mind. Tracy and I, standing under the one working light outside the bowling alley, tired and laughing and half-drunk, our first kiss and a thrill running through my body as I watched him walk away.

At home, my mom and I exchanged an exhausted, limp hug. *Don't think,* I told myself as I heard the careful click of the front door closing behind her. *Just go to bed.*

I slept better than I had in ages. I slept like the sedated, like the dead.

The next morning, I got the girls up and immediately started raving about their new fun adventure. Day care! New toys! New friends! Yummy snacks! They were so excited by my excitement that they went with it and didn't mention their dad.

I was glad for my private office that day. Though I trusted my coworkers, I was not ready to talk about what was going on, afraid that if I did, the thread of calm I was clinging to would snap. *Stuff it down, Michelle,* I told myself. Happy face. My phone rang on and off throughout the day, with nurses calling to ask questions or to get authorization for tests and more tests. They'd need to keep him for a while but soon they planned to move him to an inpatient room.

February 9: Stay through Mon.

February 10: Working on transfer.
It took Charlotte a couple of days to wonder where Tracy was. We'd just about made it out the door, lunch boxes in tow, when she stopped and asked, "Where's my daddy?"

By this time, I'd had a chance to prepare myself for this inevitable question. "Daddy is super sick," I told her. "But don't worry, he's at a really great hospital with really great doctors and nurses who are taking really great care of him."

"Can we see him?"

"Not yet," I said, then paused. My mom's sage advice for communicating difficult information to the kids was, "Shut up and say less." I finally understood what she meant. These days, we talk too much, we give kids every detail; they know when the bills are due, what happens to the bodies of beloved pets after they die. Is so much honesty good for them? Does it teach them how to talk openly about touchy subjects? Or does it put undue weight on their shoulders when they are still too young to bear it? I chose my next words carefully. "We should see him soon," I said, making no promises as I opened the passenger door to the minivan. "Daddy loves you so much, and Mommy is visiting him. He's sick but the doctors are helping him."

That seemed to satisfy her curiosity for the moment. "Let's go!" I said in my happy-chipmunk voice.

There was no time, no time, no time. So much to do, no time to do it. A necessary mania quickly overtook me. I couldn't go to the hospital every day, but thankfully, among the things I didn't have time for was guilt, at least not for this particular failing. I was there as much as I damn well could be, taking a long lunch to rush over to the hospital for a short visit, or stopping by briefly before starting the hour-long drive to pick up the girls from day care. I pounded Diet Coke to stay awake. In the evenings, I was the master puppeteer holding every damn string. What can I get done, and how could I do it hyperefficiently? Dinner of mac and cheese from a box or scrambled eggs and toast or grilled cheese sandwiches, golden brown and dripping with butter. I'd have a bite or two as I washed the dishes. Baths, books, bed. Girls tucked in, pillows fluffed and foreheads kissed. As soon as they were asleep, I made their lunches for the next day and cleaned the house like Mary Poppins on speed, a burst of energy propelling me to get ahold of a situation that was so fucking out of control.

Organization! Dishes washed and laundry folded! To-do lists, check check check!

Then I'd sit down and get high on spreadsheets. I'd started cataloging Tracy's medical treatments on February 6, 2017, the day he'd been admitted, the day after the New England Patriots broke our hearts by beating the Atlanta Falcons.

Man, I love a list. Nothing else makes the random chaos of the universe seem manageable for a moment. I was fully aware of the delusion, but the adrenaline and Diet Cokes coursing through my veins, the terror and aspartame, kept me going. If I could just get it all written down right there in a digital spreadsheet, then I'd see a pattern emerging, like those Magic Eye posters that were all the rage in the nineties. Stare at one long enough and you'll see a sailboat or a peace sign or a cure for alcoholism, a broken marriage, and pulverized life plans.

I'd get to bed at 2:00 a.m. and boy did I sleep well.

February 11: 3 mos. to live. Alcohol hepatitis. No liver transplant. GI tomorrow. Liquid/belly questionable.
On that first Saturday, my dad took Justine and Charlotte for a special day with Papa. I had a moment to breathe, to visit Tracy at the hospital without having to race back and forth or rush to the next thing.

I parked and walked inside as the sliding glass doors parted for me, then down the hall to the security kiosk. My head was foggy, and I felt like I had the worst hangover ever experienced in all of human history. Even though I was getting the best sleep of my life, every day came with new decisions to make and a fresh to-do list that, no matter my mania, could never be conquered. "Tracy Fink," I said before the guard on duty could ask, taking out my wallet to get my ID. He glanced at it, scanned my purse with the metal detector, then opened the big blue binder. "Mr. Fink has been moved out of the ICU," he said. "His room is on the second floor."

I followed the guard's directions to Tracy's new location. This room wasn't as nice; it was small and lacked a private bathroom and, instead of a sitting area, there was a crappy little chair pushed up against the wall. "Hey, hunny," I said, pulling it to my husband's bedside and taking a seat. This was my first visit when he wasn't sleeping. He was awake, but his eyes seemed cloudy, confused. His face was expressive, but when he spoke his words were muddled. This was no time to talk about us or to get those lingering questions answered, such as, What the hell happened at Peachford to land you here? He was on edge, too, but I couldn't figure out what it was he needed. He kept pushing himself up to sit and then fidgeting with the bedsheets.

Finally, Tracy fell asleep. I was sitting there staring off into space, exhaustion making my thoughts sluggish, when I heard the sound of rubber squeaking on linoleum, the background music of hospitals everywhere.

A woman stepped into the room. Her hair was wiry—that word *wiry* rose to the surface through the muck of my mind— and she looked uncomfortable. "Hello," she said after clearing her throat and giving a close-lipped smile. "I'm Stacey, the internist. Can I speak to you outside in the hall for a minute?"

For the rest of our time at the hospital, I called her Stacey the Internist. Her hair was an accurate manifestation of her personality: quirky and real, fried, a bit off.

I nodded, looked at my sleeping husband, and stood up, a buzzing sensation in my gut. She led me around the corner to a small alcove where another doctor, a hepatologist, was waiting for us. I sat down and the doctor began speaking, his hands resting on his knees and his tone gentle. Most of what he and Stacey the Internist said went right over my head—my mind was in no state to translate medical terminology. I did catch a few semifamiliar terms: alcoholic hepatitis, inflammation, fluid accumulation, transplant, outcome. I listened the best I could, one step behind as I tried to decipher this foreign language, these words that surely did not have anything to do with my husband, with me. Jaundice—I pictured his glowing yellow eyes. Confusion and behavioral changes—I recalled those nights when I'd heard him talking to himself. The nights of his paranoia, his insistence that the police were trying to break in.

Liver failure.

"What?" I said several times. "Can you repeat that?" For forty-five minutes, Stacey the Internist and the doctor explained and re-explained. "Because of the alcohol abuse and its damage to his liver," said Stacey the Internist, holding my gaze, "your husband is not a viable liver transplant recipient."

Comprehension dawned. Well, sort of. *OK*, I thought. *Tracy can't get a liver in the state he's in. So he'll get better, then get a new liver.*

I returned to the room. Tracy was sleeping, so I grabbed my purse, kissed his sweaty forehead, and left. I didn't see death's door. I didn't know what death's door looked like. He had a long road to recovery ahead of him, I believed, or chose to believe, and a lot of painful detoxing to endure. Then he'll be ready. Then he'll get well.

February 13: MRI, no results.

February 17: Speech therapist/swallowing.

February 18: Speech therapist/swallowing.
"Hi, Tricia," I said.

"How's my boy?" my mother-in-law asked.

I got right to the point. The only benefit of this new development was that Tricia would have to put aside her anger about our move or, more accurately, she had to focus on the more important issue of Tracy's health. "You need to come out here and see your son," I said. There was a moment of silence on the line. "I know you said you wouldn't visit us out here," I continued, kicking myself for jabbing this sore spot while also knowing that it had to be done. "But this is serious."

My life had hit a new level of surrealism. How was it possible that my husband had been in the hospital for almost two weeks, in and out of consciousness? How did we get here?

Life went on. Valentine's Day had passed without comment. Compression devices massaged Tracy's legs to keep the circulation moving. Gray spread into his hair; his fingernails grew out ridged and yellow. Sometimes he was unconscious, sometimes he was incredibly agitated, his body fighting through detox as he lay there immobilized. The anger and frustration I'd felt toward him for so long had dissipated. How could I be mad at this sick, helpless man writhing in a hospital bed? Sadly, we never held a "normal" conversation while he lay there. He was incapable of having a coherent discussion. Our last moments of kindness were left behind when I'd dropped him off at treatment that day after Super Bowl Sunday.

Every day, or almost every day, I updated the spreadsheet, then relayed information to Tracy's best buddies as though I were a project manager tracking a new system's development, not a wife watching her husband suffer. Every day, I'd text or call Marcelo. To save time, I'd copy and paste the same message for him, Jose, Misty, Tricia, Suzanne, and Tracy's cousin Brenda. Nurse Marcelo and physical therapist Jose were able to guide me, to translate lingo and help me make decisions.

Even with their help, it just didn't make sense, so I made a second list.

How much had Tracy drunk leading up to his hospitalization? I scoured our credit card statements and documented the money he'd spent, starting December 21, 2016, the day before the big fight at the top of the stairs, the one that Charlotte had interrupted. His vodka-buying schedule, for the most part, was every other day or every few days, with multiple trips to the store on many of the days. There were a couple of anomalies, however. He hadn't bought any Tito's from December 22 through December 26, though this was followed by three separate purchases on December 27. Maybe, the fight had scared him as much as it had scared me. Or maybe it was the more obvious retail disruption of Christmas, and probably he'd just planned ahead and stocked up. Then there was a gap from December 31 to January 3. New Year's Eve could account for that.

There were two gaps that didn't have obvious causes. One was between January 11 and January 19, and the other stretched from January 27 to February 6, on which Tracy made the final charge of $29.67. That was the day he'd checked into rehab. I paused at that one, my fingers hovering over the keyboard. Maybe he'd bought a bottle the day before, on Super Bowl Sunday, when he'd gone to the grocery store for more chips, and the charge hadn't showed up until the following day. I recalled him gulping down vodka that morning, before my mom showed up to take the girls.

Total: $422.24.

Whether the dates were a little off due to credit card or banking record delays, there was still the issue of those gaps. Maybe Tracy had simply paid in cash. Where would he have gotten cash? My job paid me with direct deposit every two weeks, and we used our credit or debit cards for everything. Rarely did I get cash back or visit the ATM. Something didn't add up. Had he been attempting a DIY detox? One quick search on the Google machine told me just how bad of an idea that was. Alcohol withdrawal is serious business and, if not done carefully, can come with all kinds of side effects, including death. Other symptoms include nightmares, seizures, and hallucinations. That last one drew me up short. Again, I recalled overhearing Tracy talking to himself late at night, and those two terrible nights when he thought the police were after him and I thought he was having a psychotic break.

I stopped there. Seeing the past few weeks in black and white was enough. I remembered our first fight in New Orleans on the way out to Atlanta, how he'd gotten in my face and refused to leave me alone until I fell out of bed while attempting to push him away. That, in my mind, was when things changed, but I hadn't noticed the details. There was too much to do and, as I'd told Tim, I had never seen alcoholism and didn't know what I was looking at. Maybe I was ashamed. Maybe I didn't want to know.

Oh God. Another thought. Had Tracy been spending that kind of money when we'd been unemployed, our savings dwindling, every trip to the grocery store to buy bananas or peanut butter a source of anxiety? Had he been spending that kind of money during that first Christmas in Atlanta when we couldn't even afford gifts? I couldn't bear it. The sadness, the anger. So many terrible questions. How had I not seen this unraveling?

February 19: Liver transplant list after 6 mos. treatment.
Tracy's parents arrived on February 20. Our first meeting here in Atlanta was formal, with a touch of ice at the edges, at least with me. With the girls, they were warm and unhurried, like it was any old visit from their loving grandparents. I helped them get settled into the guest room in our new place, and my dad offered to pick them up in the mornings to take them to the hospital. I have to work and, anyway, it's better that I'm not there. I can't watch them with their child in this state.

February 21: Ate applesauce in a.m., p.m. happy. Trying to feed through IV, no big change.
Stacey the Internist stopped by today. Since she was one of the first people to take the time to sit down with me and talk that

first week, I'd imprinted on her a bit. Her presence, her frizzy hair, comforted me, even as she was talking about feeding tubes and liver failure and lack of change. "He is not a candidate for a liver transplant," she reminded me.

Yes, I knew that. She'd already told me so. But he was still fighting hard, and I was sure he'd get a grip on this latest setback. A couple of days ago, a nurse had mentioned getting on the transplant list after six months of treatment. The next six months would suck. He'd be sick, I'd be going from day care to work to home to the hospital and round and round again. The girls and I would be living on grilled cheese sandwiches and cereal. I'd be the mommy and the daddy for a while, and then we'd get Tracy back.

I did a mental calculation. It would be around August or so, but maybe if things went really well, he could be on the mend in time for Justine's birthday in July. She'd be turning three.

February 22: New bed to relieve pressure, trying feeding tube.
Stacey the Internist came in to tell me more about the feeding tube. I nodded along, looking between her and my husband. He looked misshapen and sick as a dog; she looked sad. "His digestive tract is not functioning," she said.

"OK," I said.

"We're going to try a feeding tube to see if that helps."

"OK," I said again. "That will help him recover faster, right? Then he can start eating again?"

"Well, no," she said. "It's not just his digestive tract. It's his body. His body is not functioning. Do you understand?"

"Yes," I said. But I didn't.

February 23: Rash reaction due to one med.

February 24: Urinary infection, fever broke at 7 p.m.
At work I worked. At home, I'd put on a happy face for the kids, pop a record on, and start a dance party amid the boxes in the living room. Everything was fine! Where was Daddy? He was resting at the hospital still, and he misses you and loves you so much. I was told that no little kids can see Daddy. Tell me more about your fun day at day care!

What was I thinking? I was not so much thinking as doing, constantly moving, talking, asking questions, researching, authorizing procedures. I was the fire that races toward oxygen, the baby gazelle chased by the cheetah. I was like Dory in that freaking annoying movie my kids loved. "Just keep swimming, just keep swimming, just keep swimming." I was like a great white shark—if I stopped moving, I'd die.

February 25: Losing skin on buttocks/special lotion/fever back. TPN [total parenteral nutrition] to feed/ate dinner.
There was nothing to do but pace. It was Saturday. My mom had taken the girls for another fun day with Nana, but it was getting late, and I knew she'd be more than ready to head home. Tracy had another fever and, even worse, he'd developed bedsores. The skin on his backside was hot to the touch and looked scraped, like he'd crashed his bike and skidded on the asphalt ass first. It looked ugly, and painful.

Earlier in the day, Stacey the Internist stopped in. She read over Tracy's chart and, with a nurse, gently rolled him onto his side so that she could take a look. She pulled up his hospital gown, pursed her lips, then they returned him to his back. "Please," she said, gesturing to one of the chairs. "Take a seat."

The nurse left the room and Stacey the Internist sat down in the other chair with a sigh. "Michelle," she said. "Those bedsores are not a good sign."

I nodded. "What's the treatment?"

"The doctor will be in to see you shortly, and he'll go over treatment with you in detail. For now, I can tell you that we'll continue to shift Tracy's position as much as possible, and he'll keep wearing compression sleeves on his legs to help with circulation. Essentially, we will do whatever we can to keep your husband comfortable."

I nodded again.

"But I need you to know something." Her tone changed, from the flat, rat-a-tat delivery of explanation to gentle, careful. I looked up from my hands in my lap and into the dark brown of her eyes. "He is not a candidate for a liver transplant and, with the way things are going, he never will be. He is not going to get a new liver. He is not going to recover. Do you understand?"

I nodded, a human Pez dispenser. In the back of my mind, a light bulb was going on, but illumination was slow; a light on a dimmer switch. Slowly, slowly, understanding was dawning. Stacey the Internist stood up and put her hand on my shoulder for the briefest of moments, then left, her shoes squeaking goodbye on the linoleum.

I waited. I was tired, so tired. When had I gone to sleep the night before? I couldn't remember. My thoughts swirled around a truth but never quite touched it. *He is not going to get a new liver. He is not going to recover. Do you understand?* I waited some more. Where was the doctor? Bedsores were serious, especially with a fever, and—I checked my phone—I'd been waiting hours. Tracy was going in and out, and when he was awake, he was obviously in pain. I checked my phone again. You OK? I texted my mom.

Yes, she replied immediately. Making dinner for the girls.

Can you stay a little bit longer? I'm waiting for the doctor to check in.

Three dots, then, You bet.

More pacing. I texted Marcelo, turned up the alert sound on my phone so I'd hear when he got back to me, then put it facedown on the little chairside table next to my purse. My thoughts skittered and scattered, from home to work to my husband lying unconscious in this terrible, horrible place, his skin hot to the touch. Eventually I found a focal point, a focal sensation: anger. Where was the doctor? *You know,* I imagined telling him, *my time is valuable, too. I've got a full-time job and two little kids who need me at home. Oh, and my husband's in pain! Why don't you care? Why won't you help him?* And so on, my thoughts spiraling out, my heart rate rising. I wanted to stomp my foot like a toddler having a tantrum. I wanted to kick the wall and slam the door and punch something, punch anything, and punch, punch, punch.

The clock on the wall above the door ticked endlessly. My ears perked up at every approaching footstep; my heart sank every time the footsteps continued past Tracy's room and down the hall. I checked my phone. Nothing. I looked out the window. Nothing. I chewed my nails, ran my hand through my hair. A handful came loose. I looked at the strands, dry and lifeless. When was the last time I'd shampooed and conditioned? I couldn't remember. When was the last time I'd had a full meal, not a Diet Coke and a slice of cold leftover pizza straight from the fridge? I couldn't remember.

Time passed. More time passed. Time narrowed and constricted.

And then the light in my mind went all the way on. *Tracy is not going to get a new liver. Tracy is not going to recover. It's only a matter of time.* I understood, finally. I closed my eyes and took deep breaths. This was not part of the plan. This was not our life, his life, my life. The girls'. What about Charlotte and Justine? This was not the plan for them.

I couldn't catch my breath. Finally, I left the room and

walked over to the nurses' station. A young nurse sat at the desk, her gaze on the computer screen. I cleared my throat to get her attention. "I need to talk to the doctor," I said.

"Patient name?" she asked.

"Tracy Fink," I said through clenched teeth. My hands were shaking.

Tap tap tap on the keyboard. "Yes, I see here that he's due for a check. The doctor will be with him as soon as he's able."

"You don't understand," I said. A wave of dizziness overtook me, and I placed my hand on the counter for support. A knot had gathered in my chest. I tried to swallow; my throat was too tight. "We've been waiting hours. Please."

"I'm sorry, ma'am, but there's nothing I can do. Please return to Mr. Fink's room and the doctor will be there as soon as he's able."

A dry cough sounded behind me. I turned. The doctor!

"Doctor!" I called. He kept moving, keeping his eyes on the hallway ahead. "Doctor!" I called again. He picked up his pace.

That fucking did it. I started crying, panting, my breath hitching as I ran down the hall after him. "Doctor!" I shouted. "Doctor!"

Suddenly a different nurse was standing in front of me, holding up her hand. "Ma'am," she said. I pulled up short. She was older and stocky, more than strong enough to restrain an agitated patient or a patient's agitated wife.

"Please," I said again. "My husband—" I put my hands on my knees. I couldn't go on; I was crying too hard. "My husband—"

"Your husband," she said, her tone gentle. "We know. We want to help you, help him, but for now you need to go back to his room and calm down."

"Please—"

"If you don't, I'm going to have to call security."

That shook me out of my state. I was not someone who got

security called on them. I was polite, complacent, a person who believed in order. I nodded and stood up, then sniffled, wiped my eyes with the back of my hand, and turned back the way I'd come. In the room, I found Tracy exactly as I'd left him. Sweaty, bloated, pink with an underlying grayish hue. I sat in the chair and took a breath. Embarrassment surged through me. I closed my eyes. *Oh my God,* I thought, shaking my head.

A while later, the doctor came in. I felt another flush of embarrassment, along with a sudden and desperate desire to leave. On my personal scale of social etiquette, I'd just had an eleven of a breakdown. I'd unleashed on this man and the kind nurses who'd been taking such good care of us. The sensation of being out of control made me want to run away, to claw at my skin. Instead, I sat quietly and attempted to track what the doctor was saying. "Yes, sir, no, sir, thank you, sir" was all the response I could manage. As soon as he was gone, I left, my tail between my legs.

February 26: TPN—Lucid.

February 27: TPN—Lucid. Fever broke.
I contacted Tracy's best friends and family. "If you want to see him," I said to each in turn, "then you need to get out here soon." To Misty, I suggested the opposite. "Don't come," I told her. It would be too devastating for her to see her ex-husband and best friend like that. Better to remember him the way he was, as an active, funny, loving person.

The feeding tube seemed to be working, delivering some amount of nutrients directly into his bloodstream. The standard for "lucid" had lowered, meaning that Tracy was considered lucid when he knew who I was and had the wherewithal to ask for ice chips or water. "I'm here," I said to him throughout the visit. "I'm here."

February 28: TPN—Called around 8:30 a.m. In/out lucid, good vitals but didn't take liquid out of belly for risk of infection/too close to intestines. 4 p.m. hemoglobin dropped. Blood transfusion around 10 p.m. (1st—had 4 units), didn't sleep all night, back on meds, constrained. I texted Marcelo. No reply. I texted again. Hello? I wrote.

March 1: Bad day. Out of it, still constrained, kidneys are reacting.

March 2: Worse day. Gallbladder reacting, hands & feet doubled in size, rash darker, coughing began, belly bulbous b/c body is pushing lining out. Tracy's belly was grotesque, an inflamed globe of liquid and heat. I texted Marcelo. His responses had grown shorter, the time between them longer.

Yo, where are you? I wrote. I need you!

March 3: Nurse Jay and Dr. Lucas called at midnight (cranky). Possible cirrhosis. Possible cirrhosis? Marcelo wasn't responding, so I looked it up. Tracy's liver was losing function. Well, that's bad news. But we already knew that, right?

March 5: Neck stiffening, on respirator, Lasix 2–3 times/ day, procedure to move tubes from left side of neck to right, had to do chest X-ray after it was switched, blood taken for testing for sepsis, spinal tap for neck stiffening, 80% use of oxygen, transfusion of 2 units of red blood cells. Tracy was fully unconscious or, as I thought about it, he'd "gone under." Neck stiffening was a common symptom of cirrhosis, as was the administering of Lasix to try to reduce fluid in the abdomen. I didn't fully understand why they were giving him a blood transfusion, only that he was not getting enough oxygen, which was bad. Obviously.

March 6: ICU. Intubated, Ativan drip, medicine drip to help blood pressure (serious med) & worked off this a.m., Lasix drip for kidneys still, try tube feed, 50% oxygen needed, bronchoscopy looks normal but running cultures, trying to keep comfortable, another transfusion of red blood cells of 1 unit.

Tracy was under, but they gave him some Ativan to reduce the risk of seizures and continued with Lasix drip to help with fluid retention. He was still not getting enough oxygen, and the pulmonologist did a bronchoscopy to check for blockages and get samples of tissue, which came back normal. No infection there.

March 7: ICU. Fever broke.

March 8: ICU. Rash worsens, fever back, spinal meningitis negative. On steroids for rash. 50% oxygen needed.

I watched as two nurses took care of Tracy's hygiene. One brushed his teeth and trimmed his beard, while the other struggled with his thick yellow finger- and toenails. They had to be extra careful—accidently nicking the skin could result in a full-blown infection. He was so bloated that he was unrecognizable; you could leave indentions wherever you put soft pressure on his feet or hands.

I could see, had to see, that my husband was completely underwater. He was with us physically, yet his brain was gone. There were so many fluids in his body with nowhere to go.

March 9: ICU. Special scan and liver biopsy.

March 10: ICU. Liver biopsy at 11 a.m., 78 hrs. results, found HSV1/herpes virus caused infection.

March 12: ICU. 30% oxygen.

Today a doctor said to me, "You know this is serious, right?"

"Yes," I said. I saw red and envisioned my own two hands reaching out and wringing the doctor's whiskery neck. I saw myself bashing his head against the wall and roaring in triumph.

Instead of committing justifiable homicide, I yelled. "I've got two little girls at home. Every second I'm not with them or at work, I'm here, watching my husband—" I couldn't bring myself to say it. "You think I don't know that this is serious? No shit this is serious!"

March 13: ICU. Ultrasound of liver & gallbladder 6 p.m., liver biopsy abnormal, Dr. Hon preparing for worst.

March 14: ICU. 30% oxygen.

March 15: ICU. Brain scan 4:30 p.m., 25% oxygen.

March 16: ICU. Brain scan healthy. Antibiotics started b/c of 2nd urinary infection.

March 17: ICU. Called in p.m. and night nurse wouldn't talk w/me w/o a 4-digit code. Spoke w/charge nurse and estab one for HIPAA/PHI purposes.

March 18: On-call physician's assistant from Grady and spoke re: getting him on transplant list and very real w/ him going soonish. Discussed the need to have DNR [do not resuscitate] on file in near future. 25% oxygen use.

March 19: ICU. No response still—day 5.
The girls have not seen their daddy in forty-eight days. Children are not allowed in the ICU. Anyway, I don't want

them to remember him this way, unconscious, wires and tubes the only thing connecting him to the world.

March 20: ICU. Dr. Hon called at 9 a.m. to say his liver was not getting worse. Left msg for the dr on staff today w/either Dr. Eaton or critical care team to learn about timing of trach & liver transplant list. Dr. L explained they would not do the trach if it meant there wasn't the opportunity for him to improve. Told dr his story w/back pain led to alcohol intake and still doesn't warrant him getting on liver transplant list till 6 mos. clean. Dr. L will be with ENT dr during the trach at end of week and they'll talk to me before they do the surgery. Transfusion at some point happened during the day.

March 21: ICU. Dr. Bomeli needed verbal approval for trach this week, Patrick needed verbal approval for dialysis to begin today (5:30 p.m.), oxygen use increase to 70%, met Dr. Hon in person, Tricia & George return to TX, Jose visits for day/visits my office, helped with T getting a chest X-ray, 4 liters of liquid taken at dialysis/ended at 7 p.m., needed 1 unit of blood.

Jose flew in from Dallas and went straight to the hospital to see his old friend. We had coordinated it so that he would take Tricia and George with him to the airport and they would catch their flights back to Texas.

George, Tracy's dad, is one of those people who very much needs a schedule. He feeds the dogs, works on the car, does whatever it is retired people do. Without these tasks, he gets agitated. We knew that Tracy wasn't coming back, so they decided to say goodbye now, rather than ride it all the way to the end of the line.

The three of them stopped by my office to say goodbye before heading out. I stepped outside the building to meet them.

We didn't have much left to say to one another, so we hugged and cried. Then they left and I returned to work.

As hard as it was for me to say goodbye to my husband day by day, I could not fathom, wouldn't want to fathom, what his parents were going through. Just because Tricia's son is in his forties doesn't mean he's not her baby.

March 22: ICU. Dialysis 2½ liters, CAT scan approved w/ Shelton 1 p.m. for this afternoon.
Tracy's uncle Bruce arrived yesterday, and while he and I were visiting his favorite nephew, two nurses stood bedside with us. My husband was no longer there, just a swollen red body that hurt to look at. I felt pity and a desire for the pain to stop. He did not deserve to end his life like this. More than anything, I hoped he knew, I hoped he could feel, that there were so many people who loved him. And all I could think was, *Is this what it feels like to say goodbye?*

Nurse Ed, who'd been there since the beginning and whom I'd grown to trust, looked uncomfortable. He was such a warm person, a big man who touched Tracy with care. To distract myself, I focused on him. I asked some medical questions, which he answered tersely, leaving plenty of space for me to read between the lines. I called him out on it. I wasn't mad, exactly, just exhausted. "Why don't you just say what you mean?" I said. He responded with a knowing look and a shrug.

The room fell silent. Uncle Bruce, who was the spitting image of Tracy, shifted his weight. I closed my eyes for just a second, felt the heaviness from my head to my feet. "Ed," I said, looking to him again, "what do you do to relax from this type of job? How do you care for a stranger with such sincerity each day? How are you so good at it?"

Ed hemmed and hawed. "Oh, well, you know. I watch TV. Drink beer. Go for hikes on the weekend . . ."

I cocked an eyebrow. "And?"

"And I ride motorcycles."

I laughed. "There it is." At last. What better way to face death on the job than to face death on the road?

March 23: ICU. Trach didn't happen, got fever and on antibiotics for it, antifungal meds for issue, blood pressure down, hemoglobin bad, platelets at 61, 3 liters/dialysis.
That night, after tucking the girls in, I pulled up my old college buddy Zeb's contact and called, then turned on the speakerphone and propped the phone on the bed so I could get my pajamas on, maybe fold some laundry while we talked.

"Hey," she said. "How are you? How's Tracy? What's the latest?"

"Hey," I said. "Well, um, things aren't good. Tracy is not good."

"What's happening?"

I took a deep breath. I still couldn't bring myself to say the D-word, so I said, "The doctors say he is not going to wake up, that it's a matter of when."

Quiet on the line, then, "WHAT? WHAT DO YOU MEAN, MICHELLE?" The phone dropped away with a clunk, and I could hear screaming and sobbing. I glanced at the door to my bedroom, afraid that the sound could wake up the kids—it was closed. Zeb's voice returned, filling the room. "WHAT ARE YOU TALKING ABOUT, MICHELLE?" Sobbing. "WHAT DO YOU MEAN?"

"I know, Zeb, it's crazy." She kept crying. "I know, Zeb," I repeated. It felt good to console her, like she was my surrogate, having the reactions I couldn't yet have, reactions that were sublimated by necessity and numbness. I took comfort in her pain. "I know, Zeb," I said while she sobbed. "I know."

March 24: ICU. Dialysis/4 liters, approved paracentesis to pull out liquid from abdomen, took 5 liters.

March 25: ICU. Dialysis/4 liters, platelets 61. Time to let him go, dr talked w/Tricia and me.

I was about to walk Uncle Bruce to his car when a nurse told me not to leave the ICU. "The doctor on staff needs to talk with you," she said, her expression giving nothing away. Bruce hugged me goodbye, holding me close for an extra second, and once he was gone, I took a seat on the small couch by the window. I didn't have to wait long before a woman in a crisp, well-tailored suit, her long black hair pulled back into a smooth bun, walked in. She looked sharp but kind. She glanced at Tracy and then at me, and I moved the newspaper I'd been staring at over to my left and scooched over to make room for her. My hands were sweating, and I placed them in my lap so that I wouldn't fidget. The last time a doctor had taken the time to sit down with me it hadn't meant good news.

Again, the hem and haw. She cleared her throat, smoothed down her skirt, looked around the room. She began and then stopped, then tried again. Recently I'd come to believe that anticipation of bad news is almost as bad as the news itself, so I looked at her and said, "Talk to me like I'm your sister. Or like I'm your best friend. Give it to me straight and don't mince words."

That was all she needed to get started. "Without a new liver, your husband's body will continue to deteriorate to the point of no return," she said then paused, holding my gaze. "Your husband will not recover."

I blinked and gently squeezed my legs above the knee. I'm here, I reminded myself, in this chair, in this room, in this moment. I already knew that, didn't I? So why was it so hard to hear? "Are you telling me my husband is about to die?" I asked.

"Yes," she said. "It's common for families to have difficulty understanding that although their loved one is here and alive, it's only a matter of time. Many people have a hard time letting go, even when they know, at least intellectually, that they can't change the outcome. Some families fight the process and confuse it for care. Some families feel guilty or ashamed and think that if they keep trying, no matter how futile it is, then they won't feel so bad. So helpless."

I knew exactly what she was talking about. I'd spent many late nights worrying that Tracy's mom thought it was my fault for taking him and her grandkids out of Texas, that he'd grown so homesick and depressed that he'd turned to alcohol for comfort. Maybe part of me believed that, too. What if we'd stayed in Austin? What if we hadn't quit our jobs, or he'd lined up work before we left, so he wouldn't have become so detached and unfocused? What if, what if, what if. The what-ifs haunted me. I felt the need to apologize to everyone, for Tracy's sickness, for my inability to stop it. *I'm sorry Tracy is dying*, I wanted to say. *I did my best.* As if this were something I could control. I had done whatever I could, refusing to give anyone a reason to think I was giving up on him, that I hadn't fought for him tooth and nail. Because, if I let it, the guilt overwhelmed me. At some point, Marcelo had said that it wasn't for me to worry about, that no one blames me. My manager at work told me about Al-Anon's Three Cs: I didn't cause it, I can't control it, I can't cure it. Whenever the guilt and shame surged, I repeated that mantra.

As though reading my thoughts, the doctor continued. "There's nothing more you can do. Mr. Fink is dying. He will die soon. Maybe weeks, maybe days. There's nothing you could have done, and there's nothing you can do now. I'm so sorry."

"My husband is going to die," I said evenly. "My husband is going to die." Being realistic is different from being pessimistic, I realized. I looked at my unconscious husband on the bed. It was obvious that there was no turning back, he was too far gone, and positive thinking was not going to put a dent in reality. I could admit, had to admit, what was happening. There would be no silver linings. Death is just death, and my husband was dying.

"Have you been through this before?" the doctor asked.

I was taken aback. "What do you mean?" I said. "I don't understand the question."

"I mean, have you dealt with this type of loss before? You seem like you have."

"Oh, no," I said, trying to laugh. "Though my brother Mark did kill himself seven months ago, so there's that. Shot himself in the chest in Morgan Falls Park. But he'd been depressed for so long, and it wasn't his first attempt. In a way I was ready for it, had been getting ready for it for a while. We all had. In a way, it made sense, you know?"

She nodded.

"To answer your question, as far as having a husband die in the ICU, no. I'm a first timer." Suddenly exhaustion overwhelmed me, and I closed my eyes. *If I could just lie down right here on the couch and go to sleep . . .* I opened my eyes and rallied my politeness. "Thank you," I said, "for being honest with me. Last thing I need is false hope." Now I could prepare myself and our girls. Prepare his family and friends.

Before I left, I asked the doctor to speak with Tracy's mom by phone. It was not for me to tell her. I remembered my mom at Mark's funeral, how she'd given away the niche in the mausoleum she'd bought for herself to him, her eldest son. It was just too much for me, as a mother worrying about her soon-to-be-fatherless children, to tell another mother that her son was going to leave this earth before her. And, even in this moment, I worried that she'd blame me. But if the doctor told her the cold, hard facts, she'd have to recognize that it was out of my hands. I pulled up Tricia in my contacts and, when she answered, I said, "Hi, Tricia. I'm sitting here at the hospital. I'm with the doctor. Do you have a minute to talk to her?"

After, I gathered my things and kissed my husband good night. He did not respond.

That night, once my mom had gone home and the girls were cuddled and reassured and tucked into their beds, I looked around at the house we'd just moved into, what was supposed to be our new home. Tracy would not be returning here. Instead, I would be the safe haven, the kisser of boo-boos, the disciplinarian, the one who would be there day in and day out to take care of everything so that my kids wouldn't have to worry. I'd be the one to put bandages on scraped knees, to take them out for ice cream, to braid their hair and make them do their homework and brush their teeth and go to bed on time. I'd be the one to pay the bills, buy the groceries, put money aside for soccer lessons and physical therapy. I would be the mom and the dad.

March 26: Learned about the process, told rest of his family.
They unplugged Tracy from the machines. It was a Sunday; I chose to stay home with the girls instead of witnessing it.

March 27: ICU. Tracy passed at 11:05 p.m. EST while I held his right hand and pictures of Charlotte & Justine. Played some of his favorite music including the Flaming Lips, Depeche Mode, Iron & Wine, and Snow Patrol.
My phone rang at lunchtime. "These things happen at different speeds," said the nurse, "but there are cues. We think you should come to the hospital."

I grabbed my purse and stepped into the hallway. Around the corner, I peeked my head into the office of my manager, Karen. "I have to go," I whispered. An expression of terror came over her face and she nodded. I kept going down the hall to the office of my boss, Chris. I couldn't speak, so I gave a little wave. He nodded. They knew.

I gripped the steering wheel at ten and two. I was scared Tracy would die alone, before I could get there. For the twenty-minute drive, I repeated in threes, *Please don't go, please don't go, please don't go.* Pause, breath. *Please don't go, please don't go, please don't go.*

I parked with a jolt and raced inside the hospital. After fifty days, all the security guards knew me and waved me in without checking my ID or bag. I ran down the hall and into his room.

Tracy lay there, under a thin beige blanket, just as he had for the last few weeks. It was eerily quiet without all the machinery beeping, only a single monitor tracking his heartbeat. I watched for a moment; his chest rose and fell, the smallest of movements to signify life. Before sitting down, I straightened the photos of Charlotte and Justine that I'd left there. His girls, our girls, healthy and young and radiant. Our love and hope and dreams for the future manifest. My sweet babies. They wouldn't get to say goodbye.

It's strange, the process of dying, the hurry up and wait of it. For four hours, I sat there, waiting for my husband to leave me, with his uncle Bruce. Nothing, no change, so I left to pick up the girls from day care, to get them home and fed. On the way, I called my mom. "Mom," I said. "I need to go back to the hospital as soon as possible. Can you come over?"

"Of course," she said. "But . . ."

"But what?"

"You know, you don't need to go back there. There's nothing more you can do."

"Oh, Mom." Even in that moment, she was trying to protect me. She hadn't said much over the last couple of years about what was happening, had been there for me even as she witnessed my husband fall apart, our marriage fall apart. She is not the type to hold a grudge, to say, "I told you so." Or, for that matter, to face things directly. "Shut up and say less" was her go-to advice. This was her technique for avoiding pain, and for saving me from pain. She must have been so tired of seeing me hurt, of watching me go through the wringer. But there was no avoiding, no saving, not for this. "I don't want him to be alone," I said.

I obsessively checked my phone while I made Kraft mac and cheese, pouring the neon orange powder over the pasta and mixing in milk, and prayed for no communication. What would I do if they called to tell me he was going? Or that he'd gone? I couldn't bear it.

The kids didn't need to know what was happening. How could they possibly make sense of it? I sure as hell couldn't. I did what I do. Happy face! Nothing's wrong! Shut up and say less!

I tucked them in at 7:30 and was out the door the second my mom pulled into the driveway at 9:30. *Please don't go, please don't go, please don't go,* I chanted as I drove through the dark night to the hospital. *Please don't go, please don't go, please don't go.* Again, I raced inside. Again, I found him the same as I'd left him, unconscious and breathing shallowly, a body in a bed.

I waited in a daze, Tracy's favorite music playing softly from my cell phone. Depeche Mode, Gorillaz, the Cure. At a certain point, I asked the night nurse, "How do you do this? How do you wait for a person to die?" A sad shake of the head and a shrug was his reply.

I clutched my husband's hands, placed the pictures of the girls on his chest, stroked his hair, and whispered sweet nothings in his ear. A few minutes after eleven, the Flaming Lips' "Do You Realize??" came on.

***

Tracy died at 11:05 p.m. The nurse and I cried together. I was thankful not to be alone. I placed my hand on the photos of our children on Tracy's chest, close to his heart. "Will you keep these with him until he's cremated?" I asked the nurse.

"Yes," he said, wiping his nose with a tissue. "Do you want a priest to come in and say a few words?"

That wasn't a rite that mattered to me, or that would have mattered to Tracy. But I said yes, knowing that his mom would appreciate it. Then I waited there, next to the body that had been my husband.

Finally, the priest came in. "I'm sorry for your loss," he said. "Can you tell me a little about your husband? What were some things he enjoyed? What did you love about him?"

I blinked, letting twin tears fall. I thought back to when we first met, to that moment when I first saw him, that cute skater boy with a light in his big blue eyes. I thought about our first kiss, the way he'd looked at me when I'd walked to meet him under the arch of roses on our wedding day, the violin playing "Only You." I thought about the first time he held Charlotte, the first time he held Justine. "He would have done anything for our daughters," I said. "He was loyal to his friends. He loved going to concerts and biking. Before he got sick, he'd go to great lengths to make our lives special."

The priest nodded, then did his priest thing. "Amen," he said after reciting some prayers I didn't recognize.

"Amen," I repeated.

Death is the only way to escape logistics. Those left behind have to sign papers, answer questions, do all the things required of the living. They have to fight over two dollars with parking security. Then they go home and take care of the people who need to be taken care of. Loss is never the end—it's just another beginning.

PART FOUR

DO YOU REALIZE??

Engagement picture taken in East Austin, Texas. Spring 2011. Photo © Alison Narro

In Memory of Tracy Lindell Fink
August 17, 1971–March 27, 2017

It is with great sorrow that we inform you of the passing of our dear son, brother, husband, father, and friend.

Tracy was born on August 17, 1971, in Kingsville, Texas, to parents George and Tricia Cooper Fink. Tracy was a 1989 graduate from H. M. King High School in Kingsville, Texas, and a 1993 graduate from Southwest Texas State University in San Marcos, Texas, with a degree in marketing.

Growing up, Tracy raced BMX bikes, skateboarded, and spent time with his best guy friends, whom he remained in touch with all his life. Upon graduating from college, he relocated to Austin, Texas, where he spent the following years working as a financial analyst and gained a love for cycling and running while earning several medals for his accomplishments. Tracy, his wife, and two daughters relocated to Atlanta, Georgia, in winter 2015, where he stayed home with his girls to watch them grow. He became ill in February 2017 and passed with his wife, Michelle, by his side.

He is survived by his parents, George and Tricia Cooper Fink of Bandera, Texas; brother, Matthew Fink of San Antonio, Texas; wife, Michelle Vignault of Atlanta, Georgia, and daughters, Charlotte Cooper Fink and Justine Louise Fink. Also, aunts, uncles, and numerous cousins.

A family gathering will take place at Garner State Park and

an open-invitation celebration will be held in Austin, Texas, to unite his family and friends. The details are being worked out and those who are close will be notified once information is available. Tracy and his family spent every summer growing up at Garner State Park, playing in the Frio River. His wishes included bringing those he loved to a place he cherished. We will respect his wishes and celebrate his life.

In lieu of flowers, please write your favorite memories in a letter to Charlotte and Justine. As they grow, they can read the letters and learn more about their daddy. Please send photos and/or favorite memories to: Suzanne Valentine, ———, Austin, TX 78757.

PART FIVE

SAVE A PRAYER

Life and art intersect. Spring 2018. Photo © Michelle Vignault

April 14, 2017

Dear Pooky,

One of my greatest fears was that Tracy would die on April 1, that it would be some kind of April Fools' Day joke. Completely and utterly absurd, right? The random things we worry about. Anyway, I gave myself a few days to collect myself before asking the girls to meet me upstairs for a family meeting. We sat outside our bedrooms on the landing, seated crisscross applesauce. "This is really bad news," I told them. Justine smiled, got up, and toddled about, as she does. What does a two-and-a-half-year-old know about bad news? But her sister sat up. I took a moment to look in her eyes, to show her that I was right here with her, that I would be right here with her no matter what. "Your daddy died," I said slowly. "He won't be able to come home."

Charlotte burst into tears. I pulled her in, held her close, rubbed her little back. Justine watched us, confused. After a while she said, "Mommy? What's for dinner?"

Gawd, I love these kids.

A couple of weeks later, I experienced my first-ever weep. I'd only seen it in the movies, that moment when the spouse or parent is standing in the closet, looking at the recently deceased person's clothes, then collapses in a puddle on the floor. That's exactly how it played out for me. I hugged Tracy's shirts and buried my face in them, the sound of hangers rattling on the rod. They smelled like him, of course, and I lost it. I held on even as my knees buckled, as if it were him I was holding, and started to weep, really weep, the kind of weep with gargling sobs and moans and rivers of tears and snot. An ugly, ugly cry times ten. Once I wore myself out, I sat there and said to myself, *OK. So that's what a weep is.* And then I stood up, got out some boxes, and spent the next five hours going through his clothes and boxing them up for Goodwill. A long and awful process of deciding what goes and what stays, which shirts hold memories worth telling the girls about someday.

As I do in all hard times, I turn to organization to get me through. I've made a list, of course, not to keep tally but so I know who to thank. The outpouring of love is simply incredible. This situation is scary to so many and, in the past, I've avoided people who lost a loved one, telling myself that I was "giving them space." Yeah, right. A couple we knew years ago lost a baby at thirty-nine weeks. I did not know what to say, so I stayed tight lipped and distant. It was the love we felt for them, this sweet little family, that left us speechless and numb. What I didn't know was that there is no right thing to say, that all I had to do was show up.

We don't need space, we need no-strings expressions of love without having to ask or give instruction. I need to not have to make another decision or plan, and bless you if you can spare me one more task on the endless to-do list. I need to not have to talk about it, at least not right now. What is there to say? Just show up. Drop off bread or milk or toilet paper on the doorstep, or come inside and wash some dishes or vacuum the carpet. These little gestures mean so much.

You know I hate cooking, and my wonderful new neighbors have set up a food train to spare me that loathsome task (and save the girls from another bright-orange meal of mac and cheese). Every day I have something to look forward to when I get home and open the mailbox. Pretty cards and flowers; gift cards for groceries, toys, coffee, the movie theater, even a massage; books, stuffed animals, stickers, and games for Charlotte and Justine. Books with quirky quotes of inspiration and a crafts set all the way from Tokyo, Japan. Practically a lifetime supply of cookies. Mary, my mom's best friend from third grade, donated money to their local pediatric liver transplant program in Tracy's honor. David's setting up of a GoFundMe. It's overwhelming at times, this love, and it gets me through the day. A happy distraction, too, like Christmas morning for the girls.

Thank you for the cookies, groceries, and flowers. More than that, thank you for sticking through this with me. Thank you for visiting in February—I can't remember it at all, I was in such a daze, but I know you were here. Thank you for being by my side, my support, and friend all these years.

With gratitude,

M

May 8, 2017
Suzanne,

I've signed us up for eight weeks of group therapy sessions with some other families. I am determined to talk about this with Charlotte and Justine, now and when they get older and start to ask questions. I want to give them answers, as many as I can. The only question I won't be able to answer: Why? Why did two little girls lose their dad? Why did I become a widow? None of it makes sense, and there are no good explanations beyond the technical: Your father drank. Your father started drinking at fifteen and never stopped. Your father had chronic back pain, stopped taking good care of himself, became depressed when we moved to Atlanta, and proceeded to drink himself to death. There you go. Except that's the how, not the why. Somehow that doesn't quite cut it.

Still, I am determined to face it with them and buck the

family tradition of stuffing it down, down, down, never to be heard from again. I want to teach them self-sufficiency and independence, but would prefer to leave the loneliness and denial and fakery behind. Will that make their lives easier or harder? Only time will tell.

For the first couple of sessions, the adults went into one room to talk about grief while the kids went into another room for talking and art therapy. It was a great chance for the girls to be around kids who, like them, have lost a parent, and it gave me a chance to learn from other grievers about what was working or not for them. Two of the women had husbands who died of alcohol abuse. One was a stay-at-home dad like Tracy, while his wife was the breadwinner. She knew all about the crap I've dealt with and having to put on an actress face day in and day out. It's a relief to know there are more people (probably a lot more people) like me.

Not until you're handed a bag of shit are you able to see whether you can handle carrying a bag of shit around. In a way, I'm glad that this happened now, when I'm heading toward my midforties, and not when I was thirty or thirty-five. "Glad" is the wrong word, but you know what I mean. I have the confidence and the not-give-a-fuckness now that I didn't have when I was younger. It's OK, I can breathe, just breathe. Well, it's not really OK. I'm sad, lonely, and always tired. So, so tired. But I carry this bag of shit around with pride. I am proud of having to run a household, work full-time, raise two girls and, maybe way off in the future, have my own life, too. A life doing things that I love. No one is holding me back. Finding enough time and energy is what I need to make the life I want. Maybe someday I'll have the time and energy to ask myself, What might this new life look like?

Last month, I went to a Duran Duran concert. I'd bought tickets for me and Tracy. We'd seen them in Houston in 2010, then again in San Diego when I was pregnant with Charlotte in 2012. He wasn't a diehard Duranie like me, but he liked their music and got a kick out of my obsession.

For a microsecond, I wondered if it was appropriate for me to go. Only a microsecond. They have been my lifeline for going on forty years—forty years!—so why wouldn't I grab on to them now? I brought Matt from the docent program at the High with me, knowing that he liked them, too, and that he could handle whatever happened.

The last song of the set was "Rio," a favorite song by my boys of Duran Duran. I burst into tears.

It is such a bizarre feeling, this thing called grief. How it sneaks up when you don't expect it. Certainly when you don't want it. Recently I was sitting on my porch on a weekend afternoon with the girls while they laid out blankets and lined up toys. I made moves to join them, and Charlotte said, "Don't, Mommy! Justine and I are playing." So I sat back on the bench and swallowed the lump in my throat. My babies, growing up. I was filled with this immense sadness and, at the same time, pride. Pride in the mere fact they are loving sisters who were creating a pretend world for themselves in that moment, without me or anyone else. They are whole, the two of them, together and individually. Nothing will change that.

With love,

M

June 23, 2017

Pooky,

The kids and I were able to get through their first Father's Day without their dad. Last Friday, Charlotte came home from day care with a handmade origami craft in the shape of a men's button-down shirt and tie. "Who are you going to give this to?" I asked. "Uncle Johnny?"

"No, silly! This is for you. You're the mommy and the daddy."

My heart simultaneously broke and overflowed with love. My little girl, four-and-a-half going on fourteen. I don't know if one of her teachers talked about this with her, maybe under the inclusivity umbrella of "all families look different," but she said it with such ease. *You're the mommy and the daddy.* It's true now. I am officially an only parent. Do not call me a single parent. I did not choose to be single. There was no divorce or separation. No opportunity to discuss our future. That ended the night Tracy died in the hospital. Simply me and the male nurse crying together while I waited for the priest to say a few words of kindness. I'm not reconciled to that idea of being *single*. I am an *only* parent. Now, there is no one to tap out to when things get crazy at home. There is no "Hunny, can you bathe the kids tonight while I tidy up?"

I don't have the time or the desire to wallow. When you have littles, there are no options but to get up and go. Every morning, Charlotte and Justine wake up wanting breakfast. Every night, they go to bed wanting hugs and a story or two.

They are the reason I keep going. I know you understand. But sometimes I wonder if I'm heartless because I still look forward to going to work every morning and, as much as I love our nighttime routine, I am happy to see my bed at the end of the day. My new therapist said that I'll be fighting fires for a while, and that's OK. The bad feelings come, the grief and loneliness and sense of unfairness, but there are other things to take care of in the moment. The fact that our dreams for our family of four are gone is hard to grasp. Tracy and I will never have a chance to repair our marriage, or a chance to break up and figure out a new way to love our girls. I will never get to ask those questions I didn't know I needed to ask before. Instead, I must release the questions, the what-ifs. Release and accept.

A few weeks ago, on Easter Sunday, I helped the kids dress in their sunniest sundresses. Charlotte wore a 1950s-style number, with blue, pink, and white stripes and a bow around the waist. Justine brought more of a 1970s vibe in gingham with patches of pink-and-yellow plaid and green paisley. Midmorning, we attended the neighborhood Easter egg hunt in the shared green space near the tennis courts, pool, and playground. Then we went home to have our own egg hunt and break the cascarones that Granny sent from Texas.

We were in the backyard. Charlotte was walking up the rock steps to the second level, carrying her little basket proudly on her arm. Justine followed behind, that dreamy bounce in her gait. It was one of those simple, perfect moments, just us three, the sun shining, the birds singing, the colors cheery and bright. And I felt good, really good. They are so little, with so much time to grow. I sighed, feeling a relief I hadn't felt in so very long. If there's one thing I've learned from writing to you, Suzanne, it's that—wow!—I've been through *a lot*. I know I can't guarantee my girls that everything will be OK. But because we've gotten this far, I know that whatever happens, we will get through it.

Love always,
Michelle

EPILOGUE

June 2023

I still cringe every time Father's Day comes around. Finding ways to move forward while still celebrating Tracy's life and keeping him in his daughters' lives is a challenge every year. Charlotte and Justine will forever have a hole in their hearts from not having their father. I cannot fix that, and I cannot change that. I want to teach them their parents shared genuine love—during good and bad times—and that we can still come out of it together. That we can be a united family and continue to form positive, lasting memories.

What I can do as their parent is to provide them options and resources to manage their grief. The girls have been processing and working through the loss of their dad as long as they can remember—through group and individual therapy and open conversations at home. I have learned to become more patient with them, allowing them to take their time to express themselves. I stopped trying to put words in their mouths or rush them. "Let me say my words" is a frequent statement we use. No more stuffing things down. We're all working on articulating our emotions—even the hard ones.

The first year after Tracy's death, I was stuck in a dense grief fog. Each workday, I drove the girls to day care and escaped deeper into my job. I occupied myself with tasks, projects, meetings, and events, which provided me with a routine and sense of purpose that kept me focused—while also giving me the opportunity to ignore the hard feelings, big expectations, and pressure of being an only parent. At night, things were different. Once the girls went to bed, I was alone for the first time in the day. I was either exhausted from handing out my energy to everyone else or sailing on a natural high from überproductivity. I pictured coupled neighbors watching Netflix or Hulu together. Partners falling asleep beside their best friend. I was left with a stillness, a half-empty bed. Somehow, I endured those many sad nights. By year two, I began to overeat to drown my sorrows. I didn't, however, fall back into self-harm. I stopped hitting my legs in 2016 and haven't felt the impulse since. When my life was spinning so out of control, hitting my legs offered a sense of control over the pain I was experiencing. Writing letters to Suzanne helped me gain back more control—at least over my own story.

As the grief fog lifted over time, I began to feel a lightness and discovered my inner strength. That peace came over me and it became my superpower. To this day, I carry it with pride. The Widow Warrior has arrived! Da, na, na, na! I delved deep into YouTube and found videos on grief that spoke directly to me. I clung to the simple act of making lists. The endorphins released when you check something off a list are a real thing. It offered me a way to see that I was taking care of family needs, and it added another tool to my tool kit for beginning to take back control of my life.

- Shopping—milk, cheese, tortillas, bananas, apples, cantaloupe, Diet Coke, toaster pastries, ground beef, spaghetti, tomato sauce, red wine . . .
- Health—eye exams (we discovered Justine needed glasses in pre-K), therapy appointments, playdates, grandparent visits . . .
- Household—clean bathrooms, laundry, dishes,

bills, legal paperwork . . .
- Friends—make calls, return texts, send thank-you cards . . .

When it comes to labels, I am a widow. To this day, I don't get an evening off kid duty. No running to the grocery store to grab a few things while the family stays home. I do not get to tap out—unless, of course, there is a *lot* of planning involved. And because of that, I've become a superplanner. I schedule sitters so I can get to know myself again. For a few years, I forgot who I was. Then, little by little, I started rediscovering parts of my identity. I would go to La Parrilla to enjoy a plate of beef enchiladas, visit antique stores, or take walks with my good pals Sophia and Kelley by the Chattahoochee River. I slowed down, stopped worrying as much, and learned how to manage my anger. Along with patience, a lesson learned was gratitude. I am thankful for my thriving daughters, my parents, who are close by, great friends, and a whole second half of a life to experience.

In my healing, I discovered three phases of growth, so I created the Venn diagram that appears at the start of part 3 (since I love a good visual):
1. Your former life—what you expected to happen
2. Your new reality—what you have to face immediately
3. Your new normal—where you are today

There were countless times I would have preferred to stay in bed, cry, not bathe, remain sad, and feel sorry for myself. But you know what? When you have two young kids, you don't get to wallow or stay depressed for long. I knew how depression affects families—from Mark's lifelong struggle, from having friends with depression, and from observing the reality of other families who have been haunted by suicide. That's not to say I didn't wallow or succumb to bouts of depression. But for me, being woken up by my sweet girls looking to me for guidance, for food, for entertainment, for kissing boo-boos, for pulling together Smurf costumes at Halloween—rising to the occasion was a way for me to pull myself out of grief, again and again. Charlotte and Justine saved me repeatedly.

Last November, I planned an extraordinary weekend away to Los Angeles to see Duran Duran inducted into the Rock & Roll Hall of Fame. Their music has been my life soundtrack since I was the girls' ages. Last Christmas, we decorated their dad's artificial white tree that we store under the staircase and pull out each Thanksgiving. While we were decorating, dancing, laughing, and being together, Justine popped out one of her zingers: "This is the life!" She was so filled with obvious joy, I almost cried.

My love for Tracy is unique among the relationships in my past that have ended. In this case, I see him daily through his daughters' faces and actions. When Justine makes me laugh until my stomach hurts, I am reminded of his love of having fun and being free. When Charlotte dives into soccer, singing lessons, drama, dance, I am reminded of his love of being active and trying new things. Tracy lives on. As his daughters do. As do I.

ACKNOWLEDGMENTS

Thank you.

There are many people to thank for their friendships. Thanks to Zeb and Todd, Melissa and Mark, Serna, David, Tim, Marcelo, Jose, Misty, Karen, Sophia and Kelley, the Stratton family, Chris and Mano, and my community in Weatherstone.

Thank you to Tracy's mom and dad, Tricia and George, to Brenda and Scott, and to Bruce and Lynn.

Thank you to my mom and dad and to John, Rowena, and Sandy for your constant love and support through these hard times. Thank you to Suzanne, Shane, and Janus for teaching me what it can look like to create a loving family.

Thank you to Cathy Fyock and Anna Katz—without the two of you, this book would not have reached the finish line.

Thank you to Duran Duran, who taught me about music, art, photography, fashion, and travel. You provided us Duranies over forty years of new music. The soundtrack to my sanity, my joy, my pain. My life.

Most of all, thank you to Charlotte and Justine for giving me the time to learn how to navigate our lives. We have amazing times together and are a force to be reckoned with. We stand strong together and I cannot wait to learn what type of women you become. I love you every minute of every day.

ABOUT THE AUTHOR

MICHELLE VIGNAULT is a widowed warrior with an art degree from Warren Wilson College. She works for a tech company and spends time with her two daughters, extended family, and friends in Atlanta, Georgia. *Hold Back the Rain* is her writing debut.

You can learn more at www.holdbacktherain.com.

Printed in the USA
CPSIA information can be obtained
at www.ICGtesting.com
LVHW100624090823
754683LV00006B/85